THE

EVERYTHING®

Bartender's Book,
2nd Edition

Dear Reader,

If you're reading this letter, you probably have a minimum desire to learn how to mix one drink or a maximum desire to mix many drinks at your own home party or a local bar. I also predict that you have a sociable personality or one inside itching to come out. Well, you've picked up the perfect book to help reach your goal.

Being the bartender at a home party bar or at a local bar can be fun, but it requires some knowledge before you step behind the wood. This book gives you the information you need to get started or brush up on your mad whiskey-slingin' skills. *The Everything® Bartender's Book* is filled with everything the beginner, middlin', or expert bartender needs to know about the stylish bar and cocktail world. And if you have any questions, don't hesitate to e-mail me at *Cheryl@misscharming.com* or visit my Web site: *www.misscharming.com*.

Cheers!

Cheryl Charming

THE

EVERYTHING

Series

EDITORIAL

Editorial Director: Laura M. Daly

Executive Editor, Series Books: Brielle K. Matson

Associate Copy Chief: Sheila Zwiebel

Acquisitions Editor: Kerry Smith

Associate Development Editor: Elizabeth Kassab

Production Editor: Casey Ebert

PRODUCTION

Director of Manufacturing: Susan Beale

Production Project Manager: Michelle Roy Kelly

Prepress: Erick DaCosta, Matt LeBlanc

Interior Layout: Heather Barrett,

Brewster Brownville,

Colleen Cunningham, Jennifer Oliveira

Visit the entire Everything® series at www.everything.com

This book is dedicated to my mother, Babs.
• • •

An Everything® Series Book.
Everything® and everything.com® are registered
trademarks of F+W Publications, Inc.

Published by Adams Media, an F+W Publications Company
57 Littlefield Street, Avon, MA 02322 U.S.A.
www.adamsmedia.com

ISBN-10: 1-59869-590-8
ISBN-13: 978-1-59869-590-8

Printed in Canada.

J I H G F E D C B A

Library of Congress Cataloging-in-Publication Data
available from the publisher

Interior illustrations by Barry Littman and Kathie Kelleher.

This book is available at quantity discounts for bulk purchases.
For information, please call 1-800-289-0963.

Visit the entire Everything® series at *www.everything.com*

Contents

TOP 10 THINGS BARTENDERS SHOULD KNOW x
INTRODUCTION xi

CHAPTER 1: *History of Alcohol and Bartending* 1
An Alcohol Timeline. 2
History of the Cocktail 5
Alcohol in the Twentieth Century 7
Bartending Beginnings. 8
Behind-the-Bar Etiquette 10
Service Tips 12

CHAPTER 2: *Bartending 101* 13
The Five Drink Families 14
Bartending Terms 15
Glassware. 17
Cool Tools 20
Alcohol. 24
Mixers. 24
Garnishes. 27
Measurements Matter 30

CHAPTER 3: *Beer: The Oldest Alcohol Known
            to Man* 33

CHAPTER 4: *Wine, Champagne, Cognac,
            and Brandy* 47

CHAPTER 5: *Aperitifs, Cordials, and Liqueurs* 67

CHAPTER 6: **Vodka: The Spirited Neutral** 87

CHAPTER 7: **Gin: Gin Is In** 111

CHAPTER 8: **Rum: How Sweet It Is** 131

CHAPTER 9: **Tequila: Mexican Beauty** 153

CHAPTER 10: **Whiskey: Amber Waves of Grain** 171

CHAPTER 11: **Shots and Shooters** 191

CHAPTER 12: **Multi-Spirited Specialty Drinks** 215

CHAPTER 13: **Punches and Party,
Holiday, and Seasonal Drinks** 237

CHAPTER 14: **Starting from Scratch:
Homemade Recipes** 255

CHAPTER 15: **Mocktails** 271

APPENDIX A: **The Wrath of Grapes—
All about Hangovers** 289

APPENDIX B: **Drinking Words Through Time** 292

INDEX: 295

Acknowledgments

I raise a toast in thanks to my agent, June Clark, and all the people at Adams Media, especially Kerry Smith and Elizabeth Kassab. I'm very grateful for their hard work.

Top Ten Things Bartenders Should Know

1. The cocktail is an American invention.

2. The first known written reference to the cocktail was in 1803.

3. The first known written definition of the *cocktail* was in 1806.

4. Jerry Thomas (1800s) was the first known celebrity bartender. He traveled the world and wrote the first known bartender book, *How to Mix Drinks*, in 1862.

5. Most professions are either physical or mental. Bartending is both.

6. Bartending is not typically an entry-level position. Most positions are filled from within.

7. You don't have to memorize hundreds of recipes to be a bartender. There are only about 50 recipes to know and all the rest are spinoffs from those.

8. There are about 1.5 million bartenders in America alone and most work local bars.

9. A real martini is made with gin and dry vermouth. And since James Bond ordered a Vodka Martini in the film *Dr. No* in 1962, vodka and dry vermouth has become acceptable as well.

10. Know how to pronounce: absinthe (AB-sinth), cognac (CONE-yak), Cointreau (KWAN-troh), Courvoisier (core-VA-see-A), crème de cacao (ka-KA-o, or ka-KAH-o), and Pernod (pur-NO).

 # Introduction

Standing behind the bar is one fine place to be. As the bartender and host at a home party or in the workplace, it's your job to keep the good times rollin'—and with this book you'll be prepared. Above all, you'll be able to dip into the book for information, tips, ingredients, and recipes. You'll find everything—glassware, tools, spirits, beer, wine, mixers, garnishes, party ideas, and techniques.

The Everything® Bartender's Book, 2nd Edition, begins with a brief history of alcohol, spirits, cocktails, and the bartending profession. It goes on to give you all the basics you need to know to concoct a cocktail. You'll find that there's no great mystery to making one. You only need to grasp the differences between drink families and the basics of shaking, blending, and mixing drinks.

For the sake of understanding—and sampling—the basic contents of drinks, a chapter is devoted to each spirit that makes cocktails possible: vodka, gin, rum, tequila, and whiskey. Some of the greatest drinks ever invented are made with one liquor and one mixer, and you'll find them in their respective chapters.

If you are going to be an *Everything*® bartender, you have to be hip to what's current and wise enough to know what's classic, so this book gives you the best of what's timeless—the Whiskey Sour, Tom Collins, Old-Fashioned, and other favorites with their variations and mutations. There is a special classic symbol ¥ by each classic cocktail so that you know the difference between a mutation and the original classic. All bartenders should know these classic drinks in their basic forms.

Other chapters include shots and shooters; specialty and multi-spirit drinks; beer; wine; aperitifs and cordials; holiday drinks and punches; and homemade recipes. The shots and shooters chapter includes the hottest and hippest shooters found in nightclubs—classics, layered, flaming, and even more shots. Drinks like the Long Island Iced Tea, which contains vodka, gin, rum, and tequila, will be found in the multi-spirit chapter. The wine chapter covers recipes made from many wine-based alcohols, such as champagne, port, sherry, cognac, and brandy. Aperitifs with a wine base like vermouth bleed over into the aperitif and cordial chapter. There's even a chapter of recipes where you can learn to make, for example, your own coffee liqueur, Irish cream, faux absinthe, and more!

Finally, you'll find many tidbits peppered throughout the book—bar- and cocktail-related jokes, trivia, hints, bar tricks, and more. As a whole, *The Everything*® *Bartender's Book* provides you with a well-rounded perspective on what it takes to be a bartender. Now go out and shake things up!

Chapter 1

History of Alcohol and Bartending

Alcohol consumption dates back almost to the dawn of human civilization. Over time, alcohol developed into a major trade item. Some regions developed specialty drinks that we still drink today, such as tequila and champagne. Through it all, there always had to be someone on hand to host and serve the alcohol. The duty of tending bar truly reaches back to ancient times.

An Alcohol Timeline

No one knows the exact moment, year, century or even period when alcohol was first discovered. It's believed that alcohol has been around since at least 10,000 B.C.E. because archaeologists unearthed Stone Age beer mugs from the Neolithic period.

Ancient Alcohol

Long before the dawn of the Common Era, ancient civilizations around the world brewed and distilled alcohol using whatever ingredients were available to them. The Chinese made wine as early as 7000 BCE, and rice-based sake spread through Japan around 200 BCE. The Babylonians recorded their recipes for beer on ninety-two stone tablets in 4300 BCE, and rice and barley beer were brewed in India by 800 BCE. Archaeological evidence suggests that alcohol was an important part of ancient life. People depended on it for commerce and celebrated deities like Bacchus, the Roman god of wine.

Water into Wine

Alcohol became a common drink, but apparently it wasn't as plentiful as one happy wedding couple in Cana would have hoped. They ran out of wine for their guests, and Jesus of Nazareth performed a miraculous transformation of water into wine.

Ancient people also recognized problems associated with alcohol consumption. Alcohol had its first brush with the law in 50 BCE when King Burebista of Thrace became the first to ban alcohol. Religions from Christianity to Hinduism to Buddhism encouraged drinking in moderation, and Islam forbade it altogether.

Medieval Alcohol

The fall of the Roman Empire brought changes to all of Europe. Infrastructure crumbled, but trade still allowed new techniques and products to circulate. Around 900 CE, Viking ships disguised as *barcos rabelos*—wine merchants' vessels—entered the Douro River in Portugal. Monasteries became the keepers of alcohol; they had the resources to uphold the labor-intensive process of making it. French monks, forced inland by Viking raids, cultivated Chardonnay grapes and made Chablis wine circa 800 CE.

Medieval Innovations
Persian and Arab alchemists pioneered the conventional process of distillation in the Middle Ages, and the new types of alcohol it produced were used for medicinal purposes at first.

During the Black Plague epidemic in the fourteenth century, some people believed that drinks made from juniper berries (gin) could save them. Others believed consuming alcohol in moderation was the key to warding off the plague.

In the 1400s, so many alchemists were distilling alcohol that England's King Henry IV ruled only the monasteries could continue the practice. Meanwhile, German brewers perfected the lager method, and the first export of Russian vodka was recorded in the sixteenth century.

Alcohol in the New World

Alcohol played a large role in travel and exploration. In the New World, Columbus found Native Americans making beer from corn and black birch sap. Ferdinand Magellan, captain of the first ship to sail around the world, spent more money on sherry than weapons when stocking his ship for a voyage to the New World. Sir Walter Raleigh brewed the first beer in Virginia and then sent a request for better beer back to England. Colonists made wine from strawberries, blackberries, gooseberries, and elderberries. They also planted non-native apple trees, which yielded cider.

Tequila
The Aztecs used the blue agave plant to make alcoholic beverages long before the Spanish discovered the plant and created tequila. The first tequila distilleries opened in Mexico in the seventeenth century.

Modern Beginnings

The brands we know today began to appear on the scene in the eighteenth century. In 1759, Arthur Guinness signed a 9,000-year lease for a brewery in Dublin. The Guinness Storehouse welcomes tourists, and a tour of the Storehouse culminates with a complimentary pint of Guinness in the Gravity Bar, which provides a 360-degree view of Dublin. Richard Hennessey founded Hennessey Cognac in 1765, and across the Atlantic, the Reverend Elijah Craig created a new whiskey formula of corn, rye, and barley malt, and established the Jim Beam distillery in 1789.

History of the Cocktail

The origin of the word cocktail will probably never be known because there are many stories of where it came from. These origination accounts include a woman named Betsy Flannagan putting a rooster tail in drinks (cock-tail); an American tavern keeper pouring alcohol into a ceramic rooster, then guests would tap the tail when they wanted a drink; and a possible derivation from the French word coquetel. The very first known mention of the word "cocktail" was found in an early American newspaper, the *Farmer's Cabinet*, on April 28, 1803. It read, "Drank a glass of cocktail—excellent for the head. . . . Call'd at the Doct's. found Burnham—he looked very wise—drank another glass of cocktail."

In 1806, the definition of the word first appeared in print in the Hudson, New York, publication *The Balance & Columbian Repository* as a political stab against Democrats. It ran, "Cock-tail is stimulating liquor composed of spirits of any kind, sugar, water, and bitters. It is vulgarly called a bittered sling and is supposed to be an excellent electioneering potion, inasmuch as it renders the heart stout and bold, at the same time that it fuddles the head. It is said, also to be of great use to a Democratic candidate: because, a person having swallowed a glass of it, is ready to swallow anything else."

Keeping Cocktail History Alive
The historical cocktail has recently come back into vogue. Much of this is due to great cocktail historians and authors who are passionate about preserving the history of the cocktail. The main contributions come from The Museum of the American Cocktail (✉www.museumoftheamericancocktail.org), and Tales of the Cocktail (✉www.talesofthecocktail.com).

Jerry Thomas, the first celebrity bartender, published the first drink recipe book to contain cocktails, *How to Mix Drinks*, in 1862. He marveled at the inventiveness of the nineteenth-century world, of which mixology was a part. "A new beverage is the pride of the Bartender, and its appreciation and adoption his crowning glory," Thomas wrote in the 1876 edition. The book contained several drinks that are still familiar to us today. *How to Mix Drinks* included three different Tom Collins recipes, although the rest of the Collins family is not mentioned. Recipes for the Manhattan and whiskey sour were printed, and Thomas included what he termed "temperance drinks"—drinks without alcohol.

Alcohol in the Twentieth Century

Resistance to alcohol grew during the nineteenth century. Social conservatives worried about the effects of alcohol abuse on individuals and communities. In 1874, the first national convention of the Women's Christian Temperance Union was held. The Union promoted the movement for prohibition in the United States and tried to shut down saloons. They blamed male drinking for prostitution, child abuse, and poverty.

Prohibition

The temperance movement steadily gained a huge following worldwide, resulting in bans on alcohol. Canada, Finland, Iceland, Norway, Russia/Soviet Union, and the United States all enacted bans on alcohol in the first decades of the twentieth century. In the United States, the Eighteenth Amendment prohibited the sale and production of alcoholic beverages beginning in 1920. Nearly fourteen years and three Constitutional amendments later, Congress repealed the Eighteenth Amendment, but not before Prohibition wreaked havoc on the American alcohol industry. Breweries, distilleries, and wineries were forced to shutter themselves, damaging an emerging market. But Prohibition proved impossible to enforce. Americans continued to consume alcohol, smuggled in illegally from neighboring countries or produced illegally within U.S. borders. Speakeasies flourished; there were more speakeasies during Prohibition than there were legitimate bars before the Eighteenth Amendment went into effect.

Pop Alcohol

The American alcohol market rebounded after 1933, and the twentieth century saw floods of new products and cocktails. A fictional British agent named James Bond put a handsome face to the Martini. In Ian Fleming's original novel, Bond orders a dry Martini served in a deep champagne goblet with three measures of Gordon's gin, one of Gordon's vodka, and half a measure of Lillet dry vermouth shaken very well until ice-cold, with a garnish of lemon peel. This is the first reference to combining both vodka and gin in a Martini.

Public awareness of the dangers of overindulgence remains an issue. In 1980, Candy Lightner founded Mothers Against Drunk Drivers (MADD) after a drunk driver killed her 13-year-old daughter, Cari. The United States set the legal drinking age at 21 years in 1984.

The last two decades have seen an onslaught of new drinks. Malt beverages hit store shelves in the 1990s. Smirnoff Ice debuted in 2001 in the United States and quickly captured the market. In the world of cocktails, bartenders strove to invent quirky new drinks to keep patrons interested, aided by exotic products like Blavod black vodka.

Bartending Beginnings

There has always been a person in charge of making the beverages and serving them. In ancient times, it was a post-production job for women. The men grew and harvested the raw materials and women took the responsibility of cooking and preparing it into food and drink. As serving meals became an occupation and watering holes opened for people to gather, familiar features began to appear. Someone standing behind a structure—a barrier (bar for short)—serving food and drink has been recorded throughout history. Romans called their structures *thermopoliums*. Their bar tops had holes, and jars of alcohol were set down into the bar and served with ladles.

Media Bartenders
Today in movies, television, music, and novels, bartenders are typically portrayed providing solace to the downtrodden, offering psychological advice to the confused, supplying private detectives with info, or being the life of the party.

The Art of Modern Bartending

By the 1950s, thanks to new household-appliance technology and war-free times, women began entertaining in their homes. Lo and behold, the cocktail party came into its own. In the 1960s and 1970s, casual dining restaurant/bar chains permeated the nation, introducing sweetened froufrou drinks that resulted in the decline of bartending as an art and the incline of sales. The 1988 film *Cocktail* created a new category of bartender—one who puts on a show and entertains customers by flipping glasses and bottles.

The 1990s produced high-end beer, wine, and spirits that set the foundation for higher quality cocktails created by bar chefs and mixologists at the turn of the century. Today you'll find bartenders specializing in blowing fire, flipping bottles, dancing half-naked on a bar top, and using only fresh ingredients. There's also your reliable average Joe down the street at your local bar. Just know that the majority of bartenders are the latter.

Before They Were Famous

Many famous people tended bar—Bill Cosby, Bruce Willis, Sandra Bullock, Dave Matthews, and Ellen DeGeneres, to name a few. Others, like Brad Pitt, Mariah Carey, Jennifer Garner, Kevin Bacon, and Jennifer Aniston, were servers, but probably would've become bartenders if they hadn't been discovered.

Behind-the-Bar Etiquette

Being behind the bar is like living in a fishbowl. Some refer to it as being on stage. Basic bar etiquette applies to the real-world bartender and the home-party bartender.

The Real-World Bartender

The best real-world bartenders make an art form out of their profession. Successful professional bartenders possess many skills and personality traits.

- A good personality and an ability to interact well with people are two of a bartender's best assets. A sense of humor is invaluable.

- A well-groomed appearance helps bartenders seem more approachable and professional.
- Physical strength is required for long hours standing behind the bar and lifting heavy boxes.
- Basic math skills allow bartenders to make change and measure drinks accurately and quickly.
- Bartenders need to be able to remember everything from drink recipes to customers' names.
- Multitasking is a must! Bars are busy, and the bartender must make sure everything runs smoothly.
- A great smile is key since bartenders smile a lot.

Bartenders must be aware of everything around them at all times. They know the drink levels of everyone's beverage, and they see new customers as they approach the bar. A second set of eyes in the back of their heads would be a remarkable evolutionary improvement; failing that, bartenders need to be constantly alert.

The Home-Party Bartender

The bartender can literally make or break a party. Since cocktails are complimentary, private-party bartenders must be very organized with plenty of backup. Overall, they can relax and just be the life of the party because the hassle of running tabs and dealing with credit cards is nonexistent. The home-party bartender's main job is to smile, be happy, and set the tone for the party.

Service Tips

There are thousands of tips a bartender can learn through the years to help make her job easier and more efficient. There are far too many to list, but a few will illuminate the way.

- When a guest sits at the bar, always greet him with eye contact and a smile as you lay down a cocktail napkin. If you cannot get to him right away, let him know that you'll be right with him. Guests don't mind waiting if they are recognized.
- Keep the bar top clean for customers.
- Always think of sanitation. Don't let your fingers touch drinking surfaces—the top of the straw, the rim of a glass, the ice, and the top of beer bottles.
- When you are given a tip, always make eye contact and say thank you.
- Always serve the woman first, then the man. If a group of women are at the bar, it's customary to serve the oldest first and so forth.
- People love to hear their names. Try to remember names.

Chapter 2

Bartending 101

Bartender (bär' ten dur) n. One who mixes and serves alcoholic drinks at a bar, lounge, or tavern. Also called barkeeper, barkeep, barmaid, barman, tavern keeper, whiskey slinger, mixologist, and tapster. Bartending basics start with the lingo. It's also essential to recognize the glassware. The next things a bartender needs are the proper tools to make the cocktail: ice, alcohol, mixers, and the crowning touch, the garnish.

The Five Drink Families

It can be mind-boggling for the bartending newbie to glance through cocktail recipes, but they really only break down into five categories—juicy, creamy, sour, hot, and carbonated. There are a few extensions from the categories, notably the tropical, highball, stick, and classic variations.

Juicy: Juicy drinks are made with any type of juice. Popular examples are Screwdriver, Cape Cod, and Bloody Mary.

Creamy: Creamy drinks use cream, half-and-half, Irish cream, and similar liquids to give them a heavier texture. Popular examples are White Russian, Mudslide, Creamsicle, Grasshopper, and Bushwhacker.

Sour: Sour drinks are made with the tang of citrus juice. Popular examples are Whiskey Sour, Amaretto Sour, Tom Collins, Margarita, Sour Apple-tini, and Long Island Iced Tea.

Hot: These are made with coffee, hot apple cider, tea, hot chocolate, and other popular hot beverages. Popular examples are Irish Coffee, Hot Toddy, Keoke Coffee, and coffee liqueur and coffee.

Highballs

Originally, when a guest walked up to the bar and asked for a highball, the bartender grabbed a bottle of rye whiskey and mixed it with ginger ale. Today a highball just means a drink containing a spirit mixed with a carbonated mixer.

Carbonated: Carbonated drinks take advantage of soda's fizzy bubbles. These are basic highballs like Vodka and Soda, Vodka and Tonic, Gin and Tonic, Rum and Coke, Bourbon and Coke, and Seven and 7.

Bartending Terms

If you grasp these techniques, you'll be able to stand proud behind the bar with confidence.

Blended Cocktail: This is the type that you mix in a blender. Some people call it a frozen drink. The trick is to not put too much ice into the blender in the beginning; you can always add more to reach the desired consistency.

Built Cocktail: This one is the easiest to make. Start with a glass of ice. Pour in your spirits and follow with the mixer. You're done. You've made a drink "on the rocks."

Chilled Cocktail: Pouring a cold drink into a warm glass is not a crime, but it should be. If refrigerator or freezer space allows, squeeze the glasses in along with the ice cream. If not, fill a glass with ice and water just before serving.

Flamed Cocktail: The most popular flamed drinks are topped with 151 rum, taking advantage of its flammability. Always take extreme caution when handling fire, and make sure a flame been blown out before consuming the drink.

Float: To float means to pour some alcohol on top of a drink. The float adds flavor and character to a drink. Don't confuse it with the layered drink. The quantity of alcohol used in a float is less than that required for a layered drink. About half an ounce will suffice.

Layered Drink: Different types of alcohol have different weights (densities). This allows them to be layered on top of one another. For shots, you simply pour the spirit onto something like a bar spoon to break its fall so that it goes into the glass slowly. This way it layers on top of the spirit layer below it.

Muddled Cocktail: To muddle, you crush your ingredients to release their flavors.

Neat Drink: Neat means that you are pouring straight out of the bottle at room temperature.

Rolled Cocktail: You roll a cocktail by building a drink and then shifting it back and forth once with another glass or shaker tin.

Shaken Cocktail: You shake a cocktail by putting ice and your ingredients in a shaker tin and shaking the drink to make it cold.

Strained Cocktail: You are chilling the drink and straining it over ice or straight up. The most popular use of this method is with straight-up shots and shooters and novelty Martinis. The term "straight up" refers to something that is chilled.

Stirred Cocktail: One stirring technique is to build a cocktail and then stir it with a straw. The other way is used when you're making a classic Manhattan or Martini: You fill a bar glass (pint glass) with ice, pour in your ingredients, stir with a bar spoon, and strain.

Glassware

In some cases there are essential reasons for the choice of glass. A cocktail glass is held by its stem so the hand does not warm the drink. A brandy snifter is rested in the palm, so the hand does warm the liquid and release its aroma.

The pint glass can also be used as a mixing glass. or all-purpose glass. Beer, specialty drinks, sweet teas, or tropical drinks may all be served in a pint glass. Beer can be served in a mug, pint glass, stein, pilsner-style glass, yard, goblet, pitcher, or tankard. All are best chilled.

Brandy snifters range considerably in size, from 5 to 25 ounces, so use your personal preference as a guide. The brief stem allows your hand to warm the brandy. The mouth of the snifter, narrower than the base, holds the aroma. Cordials and liqueurs can be served in them, as well as high-end single malt Scotch, whiskey, rum, and tequila.

Champagne is served in either a 4- to 6-ounce stemmed, wide-mouthed glass (coupe) or a 7- to 10-ounce flute, and the style does make a difference. The open surface of the wide-mouthed glass allows the carbonation to escape, while the narrow flute preserves the bubbles. There are also two styles of flutes, called tulip and trumpet (named for their shape).

The cocktail glass (martini glass) is the symbol of drinking establishments throughout the world. It holds the ingredients over a wide surface so they are least likely to separate. The stem gives you a good grip without putting your hand to the glass and warming the drink.

A highball glass, the most universally used glass, holds 8 to 12 ounces of on-the-rocks drinks like Scotch and Soda or Gin and Tonic. It's the glass of choice for everything from Planter's Punch to a Bloody Mary. Many bars carry the shorter highball glasses.

The Irish coffee mug is a soul-warming glass container for all hot drinks. At 8 to 10 ounces it offers enough volume for the right proportions of spirits and nonalcoholic ingredients, and its handle allows you to hold the glass while the drink is still properly hot.

Irish Coffee History

Joe Sheridan, an Irish airport bartender, invented the Irish Coffee at Shannon Airport in Ireland. In 1952, a San Francisco reporter named Stanton Delaplane took the recipe back to Jack Koeppler, who owned the Buena Vista Cafe. Today, the bar claims to serve 2,000 Irish Coffees a day.

A 1-ounce **liqueur glass** is also known as a cordial glass or a "pony." You'll find them in different shapes, but they all hold one ounce of liquid.

The **old-fashioned glass** is for the venerable Old-Fashioned, but it's also used for most cocktails when they are requested on the rocks. That's the story behind its alias, the rocks glass. Ranging from 4 to 8 ounces, the old-fashioned is the short, squat member of the glass team. A lot of bars will use this glass for their highballs.

A 3- to 4-ounce **sherry glass** holds many of the before- and after-dinner drinks, such as sherry, port, and various aperitifs. These are, by definition, small drinks, and the size of the sherry glass is right for the portion.

The 1- or 2-ounce **shot glass** does double duty as a measurer and a serving glass. Many bars don't use shot glasses as much anymore because they tend to get stolen.

The 8- to 10-ounce **red wine glass** is balloon-shaped; the 6- to 8-ounce **white wine glass** is quite a bit slimmer, but there's no need to be a stickler about these dimensions. Unless perfection is a prerequisite, all-purpose wine glasses are acceptable. Most bars use one all-purpose wine glass.

Cool Tools

Bottom line, equipment matters. No matter what your profession, the right tools are a must. Bartending is no exception. You wouldn't use your bare fingers to knit your mother a scarf, nor should you use them to strain her Martini. If you are equipping a home bar, think about the drinks you and your guests like the most and prioritize which tools to purchase.

Bar spoon. A bar spoon is used to stir classic Manhattans and Martinis and other cocktails in a mixing glass and to layer drinks. To layer, simply break the fall with the spoon or pour the alcohol down the spiral.

Blender. A bar without a blender is a bar without frozen Daiquiris. The heavier the motor, the better for crushing ice.

Corkscrew. The most professional corkscrew (wine tool) is the "waiter's" version, a two-in-one gadget that opens wine bottles and beer bottles. This is the only corkscrew a real bartender uses. Here's how to use it to open a wine bottle: Remove the foil around the top of the cork with the knife on the corkscrew. Insert the screw (worm) into the center of the cork and twist until it's nearly all the way into the cork. Set the pry bar on the lip of the bottle and pry the cork straight up out of the bottle. The knife will also come in handy for many things when working as a bartender.

Waiter's version

Wingtype

Ice scoop. An ice scoop is very important. A 24-ounce scoop is your best bet because it keeps nasty bacteria-infested hands out of the ice. Always stab the scoop into the ice handle-up so that you're only touching the handle. Never underestimate the power of ice. It's the second thing you need when making a cocktail. It's needed to melt the necessary water into the drink as well as keep it cold. The ice needs to be extremely clean at all times (preferably made from filtered water).

Jigger. This measuring device is double-sided with different measures on each end. The most popular has 1½ ounces on one side and ½ ounce on the other, but you can buy many other sizes to meet your needs.

Juice extractor and citrus reamer. Fresh juice is a small effort that goes a long way. An extractor or a reamer is the most common way to get fresh juice behind the bar when making a cocktail to order.

Mixing glass. This clear pint glass is used to make classic Martinis and Manhattans (or any stirred cocktail) and used to muddle. It can also be used as one of the pieces of a Boston shaker.

Muddler. This stick can be made of wood, plastic, or a combination of materials. It's used to crush mint, sugar, fruit, and herbs.

Pour spouts. Pour spouts are pushed into bottle openings, allowing you to speed-pour your liquor and liqueurs. They are essential when tending bar or else you would be screwing caps off and on all night. After a party at home, simply take them out and put the caps back on the bottle.

Shaker tins. There are two types of shaker tins: cobbler and Boston. The cobbler shakers consist of three pieces—a tumbler, a lid with a built-in strainer, and a cap to cover the strainer. These are popular among amateur bartenders because they are easy to use, but busy bartenders favor Boston shakers. The Boston shaker consists of two pieces that fit inside each other. One piece is stainless steel, and the other piece is either a smaller stainless steel tin or a mixing glass. You shake your drink, then tap where they meet to break the seal and pour the drink. The two-part design allows for quicker pouring.

Strainer. There are three types of strainers: the Hawthorn, the julep, and a conical mesh strainer. The handheld mesh strainer is used as a double strainer. The Hawthorn has a coil around it and is used with a shaker tin. The julep strainer is place in a convex position inside a mixing glass.

Zester. A zester (also called a channel knife) makes long curly twists. Simply set the zester on the citrus fruit, apply pressure, and slice off a long piece.

Alcohol

Marines, Boy Scouts, and bartenders should always be prepared. Stocking a bar should be a matter of personal taste, lifestyle, and finances. But unless having a drink is always going to be a solitary pleasure, the person behind the bar should be prepared for guests. How prepared is up to you. If Uncle Michael, who always visits at Christmas, only smiles with a glass of Irish whiskey in his hand, buy one bottle. If cognac inspires camaraderie among your friends, make the investment. If beer does the trick, stick to what works. Here are two suggested lists, one for a basic home bar and another that goes beyond basic to complete.

Basic Bar	Add for Complete Bar
Bourbon	Armagnac
Brandy and Cognac	Canadian Whiskey
Gin	Dark and/or Spiced Rum
Rum	Citrus-flavored Vodka
Scotch	Gold Tequila
Tequila	Grappa
Vodka	Russian Vodka
Whiskey (Irish)	Single Malt Scotch
Blended Whiskey or Rye	

Mixers

Mixers provide the flavor and balance that combine with liquor to give a drink its distinctive taste. Mixers range from plain water to club soda, from flavored sodas (like cola and lemon and lime) to fruit juices (orange, pineapple, cranberry, grapefruit, and tomato), and others. When it comes to mixers, fresher is always better.

Popular Mixers
Orange juice, cranberry juice, pineapple juice, grapefruit juice, lemon and lime juice, Bloody Mary mix, strawberry mix, olive juice, V8 juice, tomato juice, simple syrup, grenadine, coconut cream, honey, gomme, orgeat, lime juice cordial, hot sauce, Worcestershire, beef bouillon, Clamato juice, clam juice, milk, cream, half-and-half, ice cream, hot chocolate, unsalted butter, egg nog, egg white, all sodas, coffee, espresso, tea, and hot water.

Sugar

Sugar is a powerful partner in many drinks, but its presence is behind the scenes, never tasted distinctly, and never, never felt as granules. Unless granulated sugar is specified, confectioner's sugar, referred to in this book as fine sugar, should always be used. Some bartenders go a step further and prepare a "simple syrup" of sugar and water to use instead of dry sugar. To make a simple syrup, heat 2 cups of water in a saucepan and slowly add 2 cups of granulated sugar until it is completely dissolved. Boil for 5 minutes and then cool. The syrup can be stored in a bottle in a cool place.

Get Fresh!

With this book's bias for "fresher is better," it is difficult to be objective. Fresh ingredients make a difference you can taste, but it may not be possible for you to make all of your own mixes. You can buy prepared mixes for Daiquiris, Margaritas, and, of course, Bloody Marys, among others. They come in bottled and powdered form. Some are excellent and some are not. Let the bartender beware and be the judge. "Sour" mixes, which contain lemon juice, sugar, and some egg white, are a special case. Whenever a recipe in this book calls for sugar and fresh lemon or lime juice, sour mix can be substituted in the amount indicated on the product's label.

Be Bitter!

While the sound of "bitters" is not appealing, the little bottles are a witch's brew of roots and barks, berries and herbs. Bitters add a kick of flavor to the mixed drinks they accompany, always in small amounts—dashes, to be approximately exact. The most common type of bitters is angostura, made in Trinidad. Two that are sometimes used are Peychaud's, from New Orleans, and Regans' orange bitters. Bitters do have an alcohol content and should not be served to anyone who abstains totally. Tasting them plain is not recommended either.

Condiments: The Little Things in Life

Sugar and spice and everything nice are all needed at the bar. Drinks are a delicate balance of ingredients, a microcosm of flavors. When the drink that is being created only totals three to eight ounces, every dash, splash, and fraction of a teaspoon counts. Condiments are like the little things in life—they make all the difference. Stocking the bar with them is not an exaggerated effort, but as basic as buying the liquor. For some people, a Martini does not exist without an olive, a Margarita is naked without its salt. A Gibson is, in fact, defined by its cocktail onion. A collection of condiments is dependent on personal needs. The accompanying list includes items like celery stalks and horseradish for Bloody Marys that you cannot keep at the bar waiting but must be available when the drinks are made. However, kosher salt for Margaritas can be ready at any time. Here are some condiments you can try:

Sugar	Celery salt	Cloves
Brown sugar	Pepper	Cinnamon
Raw sugar	Chili pepper	Spicy seasonings
Powdered sugar	Cayenne pepper	Kosher salt
Sugar cubes	White pepper	Coconut flakes
Salt	Cocoa powder	Nutmeg

Garnishes

The most popular garnishes are the lime, lemon, cherry, and olive. Runners-up are the orange, pineapple, cocktail onion, celery, mint, strawberry, and banana. You'll see other garnishes mentioned in this book, but you'll have to go out and explore to find some of the most outlandish. Pickled okra, edible pearl dust, and oysters on the half shell have all been used as unlikely garnishes.

Cutting garnishes can be intimidating for some people but it's really easy. Just make sure you always wash your hands well first or wear rubber gloves when handling garnishes. After making a cut, always lay the flat side of the fruit down to create a stable base for cutting.

The Wedge. To cut the essential wedge, slice a lime (or lemon) in half lengthwise and cut each half into four wedges. When serving, squeeze the juice into the drink, rub the fruit side around the rim of the glass, and drop the lime in the liquor.

The Slice. If you prefer to set the lime on the edge of the glass, cut the fruit into eighths and make a slit in the meat of each slice.

The Twist. There are a few ways to make lemon twists. One is to cut off both ends of the lemon so the fruit shows. Make a slit in the fruit from end to end. Squeeze a bar spoon beneath the skin and scoop out the fruit. Cut the peel widthwise into quarter-inch strips. Another technique is to cut slits all around a whole lemon and cut off one end. You can then peel off a twist to order. The proper way to garnish with a twist is to twist the peel, colored side down, over the drink, so the oils will release. Then, rub the colored side around the rim and drop the twist into the drink. Using a zester can make a long curly twist. Simply set the zester on the lemon, apply pressure, and slice off a long piece.

Sometimes guests will ask for a soda water with a twist. This means that they want a lime wedge and not a lemon twist.

The Quarter. Quarter cuts work best when muddling. Cut the fruit in half through the middle. Lay both pieces flat and then cut twice, making a cross. This will yield four quarters per piece.

The Wheel. Cut off the ends of the fruit, then cut a ¼"-deep slit lengthwise (this slit makes it easy for you to set it on the rim of the glass). Hold the fruit firmly and cut 4 or 5 wheels.

Cutting Tools

A serrated knife is the best knife to use when cutting garnishes, and a cutting board that is not used for cutting meat is preferred. As a safety precaution, place a wet bar towel under the cutting board to avoid slippage.

The Zest. The zest is the cut that really helps you show off. It's an oval-shaped rind slice from a piece of citrus that can be squeezed over a drink and combined with a flame to make an attention-getting burst. This happens because the oil of the rind meets the flame. The most common fruit rind used is from an orange. Don't confuse this with zesting a peel, a common technique in cooking and baking. That type of zesting requires a tool called a zester, and we shall speak of it no more.

Rimming

Glass rims can be dipped in something wet or sticky and then dipped into something edible. They always make a great presentation. Margaritas look better with kosher salt around their rim and Chocolate Martinis are appetizing in a chocolate-rimmed glass.

Drinking glasses can be rimmed with sugar of all types and colors, salt of all types and colors, cocoa powder, hot chocolate powder, shaved chocolate, coconut flakes, Pop Rocks, sprinkles, edible gold flake, Cajun spices, crushed Oreo cookies, crushed graham crackers, and anything your imagination can conjure up.

Measurements Matter

Since the metric system measures the world, except in the United States, here are some equivalents and charts to help avoid confusion. When measuring ingredients for a drink, remember that the balance is important, so for weaker or stronger drinks, adjust all of the components accordingly.

BARTENDER MEASURES

Bar Measurements	Standard	Metric
1 dash	⅟₃₂ ounce	0.9 milliliter
1 splash	¼ ounce	7.5 milliliters
1 teaspoon	⅛ ounce	3.7 milliliters
1 tablespoon	⅜ ounce	1.1 milliliters
1 float	½ ounce	22.5 milliliters
1 pony	1 ounce	29.5 milliliters
1 jigger	1½ ounces	44.5 milliliters

BARTENDER MEASURES CONTINUED

Bar Measurements	Standard	Metric
1 cup	8 ounces	257.0 milliliters
1 pint	16 ounces	460.0 milliliters
1 quart	32 ounces	920.0 milliliters
1 gallon	128 ounces	3.78 liters

METRIC SIZES FOR SPIRITS AND BEER AND WINES

Name of Container	Standard	Metric
split	6.3 ounces	187.0 milliliters
half	12.6 ounces	375.0 milliliters
fifth	25.3 ounces	750.0 milliliters
quart	33.8 ounces	1 liter
magnum	50.7 ounces	1.5 liters
jeroboam	101.4 ounces	3 liters
nebuchadnezzar	20 –750 milliliters	15 liters
keg	7.75 gallons	29.3353 liters

These measures are great to look up when having a cocktail party. Experienced bartenders—through repetition—learn to eyeball everything, but if you are in doubt, then there's nothing wrong with measuring. The main things to keep in mind are that you can get 3 or 4 servings from a bottle of wine, 20 to 25 shots of alcohol from a fifth, and 30 to 35 shots of alcohol from a liter.

Chapter 3

Beer: The Oldest Alcohol Known to Man

Man has been brewing beer since the moment he remained in one place long enough to grow grain. Scientists and archaeologists tell us that beer dates back to 7000 B.C.E. Ninety-two Babylonian tablets have been found with beer recipes carved into them, and over twenty types of beer recipes have been found on Sumerian tablets. Beer was used for food, medicine, and bartering and was key in ceremonies and celebrations.

Beer History

The Egyptians were the first to refine the texture and taste of beer. After that, the Greeks and Romans carried on the beer-making tradition when there weren't grapes to make wine. Ancient Germans (Teutons) took their beer very seriously, even using it as a sacrifice to their beer gods.

During medieval times, monastery monks focused intently on making the best beer possible. Hops were first used in the 1000s, and it must've improved beer tremendously because priests baptized children with the beer made with it. By the 1200s beer was classified as ale (top-fermenting) or lager (bottom-fermenting). Germany brewed cold-temperature lagers, storing them in caves, while England brewed room-temperature ales and stored them in cellars. In 1519, the Reinheitsgebot Law was enacted in Bavaria, Germany, requiring that all beer be made only from malt, hops, yeast, and water. By the mid-1500s a way to bottle beer with a cork was perfected, the most popular song was "John Barleycorn," and there were over 17,000 taverns in England alone.

In 1978, U.S. President Jimmy Carter signed a bill legalizing home brewing of beer for the first time since Prohibition. People began experimenting, making their own home brews. Handcrafted beer combined with a high-tech era resulted in microbrews. Microbreweries sprouted up all over the country. The Institute for Brewing Studies reported explosive growth in this industry in the 1980s—and that growth was based on smallness. The comparison of these beers to the corporate kind is to liken a hunk of rich-textured, whole-grain, home-baked bread to a slice of supermarket white. Words like tangy, full-bodied, robust, and flowery have real meaning in this context. There are microbreweries in most states now.

> **The Two Types of Beer**
> Beer is classified as ale or lager. Types of ales include stout, porter, bitter, wheat, lambic, brown, pale, belgian, barley wine, amber, and cream. Types of lagers include bock, dry, light, ice, pilsner, and malt.

Beer Recipes

The term *beer cocktail* is incorrect because the definition of a cocktail means that it has a spirit base. The proper term is *beer recipe* or *beer mix*. People who are devoted to their beer might find it hard to imagine that a brew can team up with anything but pretzels and potato chips, but in fact beer makes a fine partner to many other mixes, spirits, and liqueurs.

Ale Punch

14 ounces ale	¼ ounce simple syrup
½ ounce brandy	dash ground cloves
½ ounce sherry	lemon slice

Pour the brandy and sherry into the ale then add the simple syrup, ground cloves, and lemon slice. Gently stir.

Beer Buster

2 ounces vodka
14 ounces light beer

Start with both the vodka and the beer chilled. Pour the vodka into a chilled mug and add the beer.

Bee Sting

12 ounces dark beer
3 ounces orange juice

Pour the orange juice into the beer. Stir gently to mix.

Black and Tan

8 ounces pale ale   8 ounces stout

Pour the pale ale (like Bass) into the glass and slowly layer the stout (like Guinness) on top of the ale to create a layer. Use a spoon bowl to break the fall (bars with stout on tap come with black and tan spoons).

Blackberry Zima

12 ounces Zima
1 ounce blackberry brandy

Pour the Zima over ice. Add the blackberry brandy and stir.

Black Velvet

6 ounces champagne or sparkling wine
6 ounces stout or dark porter

This was invented in honor of Prince Albert after he died at age 42 in 1861. You simply float the chilled stout on top of chilled champagne. Do not stir.

🍸 Bloody Beer

14 ounces lager
2 ounces Bloody Mary mix

Pour the Bloody Mary mix into the beer. Embellish with a dash of Tabasco and a dash of Worcestershire if you like.

Blow My Skull Off

15 ounces stout   dash cayenne pepper
1 ounce rum   lime slice

Pour the rum into the stout. Sprinkle the cayenne pepper in and mix gently. Squeeze the juice from the lime and drop it into the beer.

🍸 Boilermaker

15 ounces light beer
1 ounce whiskey

Combine the beer and whiskey in a beer mug using your preferred method. Emily Post would sip this drink after pouring the shot into the beer (pinky finger raised). Other people might drop the shot, glass and all, into the filled beer mug and chug-a-lug before the foam hits the floor.

Broadway

11 ounces light beer   5 ounces cola

Combine the beer and the cola gently because both are carbonated. This is a popular mixture in Japan.

Caribbean Night

1 ounce coffee liqueur   15 ounces light beer

Pour the coffee liqueur into the beer. Stir gently to mix thoroughly.

Cheeky Tractor

1 ounce Irish cream   8 ounces dark beer
½ ounce sambuca

Pour the Irish cream and sambuca into a glass. Fill with the dark beer.

Corona Limon

16-ounce bottle of Corona
1½ ounces Bacardi Limon

Pour out a little of the beer from the bottle, then add the Bacardi Limon.

Corona with Training Wheels

16-ounce bottle of Corona   kosher Margarita salt
lime slice

Rub the lime on the neck of the Corona bottle to moisten. Sprinkle kosher salt on the neck. Push the lime into the bottle. Lick salt before or after you take a sip.

The Five Steps in Making Beer

(1) Harvest barley and soak it, allowing it to germinate to create malt. (2) Clean and grind malt, then optionally mix it with corn grits; cook to create wort. (3) Boil wort with the herb hops. (4) Cool wort and add either top- or bottom-fermenting yeast. (5) Add flavors, filter, and pasteurize. Store in cans, bottles, or kegs.

Depth Charge

2 ounces peppermint schnapps
14 ounces light beer

Pour the chilled peppermint schnapps into a frosted mug. Top off with beer.

Dog's Bollocks

8 ounces lager
1 ounce melon-flavored vodka
½ ounce lime juice cordial

Pour the vodka and lime juice cordial into a glass of lager.

Dr. Pepper

1 ounce amaretto
¼ ounce grenadine
½ ounce 151 rum
14 ounces light beer

Pour the amaretto, rum, and grenadine into the beer.

Florida Sunshine Beer

12 ounces light beer
3 ounces orange juice
½ ounce simple syrup

Pour all ingredients into a glass and mix gently.

Hot Beer

14 ounces light beer
1 ounce cinnamon schnapps
½ ounce grenadine

Pour the beer, cinnamon schnapps, and grenadine into a glass. Slightly stir.

Isar Water

1 ounce blue curaçao
2 ounces apple juice
13 ounces wheat beer

Chill all of the ingredients. Pour the curaçao and apple juice into a glass. Fill with the wheat beer.

Lager Characteristics
Bock: can be light or dark in color but always has a hoppy taste and a high alcohol content. Pilsner: light colored (yellow) and light-bodied. Dry: light in color and body with a clean crisp taste. Ice: light in color and body with a high alcohol content.

▼ Lager and Lime

16 ounces light lager (pilsner)
½ ounce lime juice cordial

Add the lime juice cordial to the lager. Examples of a pilsner are Budweiser, Coors, and Miller.

Liverpool Kiss

15 ounces dark beer
1 ounce crème de cassis

Pour the crème de cassis into the dark beer. Stir gently to mix.

Mexican Cherry

16-ounce bottle Corona
½ ounce grenadine
1 maraschino cherry

Pour out a little of the beer from the bottle. Add the grenadine and garnish with a cherry on top.

Michelada

7 ounces light beer
1 ounce tequila
1 ounce lemon juice
dash Tabasco
dash Worcestershire
pinch of salt and pepper

Pour the beer into a glass filled with ice. Add the tequila, lemon juice, Tabasco, Worcestershire, and salt and pepper.

Orange Spiked Lager

1 ounce orange liqueur   15 ounces light beer

Pour the orange liqueur (like Triple Sec) into a glass. Fill with beer. To make the beer appear green, replace the orange liqueur with blue curaçao.

Passion Beer

14 ounces light beer   ½ ounce passion fruit juice
1 ounce passion liqueur

Pour all ingredients into a glass. Gently mix.

Ale Characteristics
Stout: very dark (almost black) with a very full body. Brown ales: medium-bodied, buttery, and smooth. Porter: dark and hoppy. Wheat: light, creamy, and fruity. Pale ale: medium-bodied with a slight bitterness. Cream ale: light-bodied with a malty flavor. Amber: medium-bodied and hoppy.

Peach Spiked Brew

1 ounce peach schnapps   15 ounces light beer

Start with both ingredients chilled. Pour the peach schnapps into a glass. Fill with beer.

Red Eye

2 ounces tomato juice   14 ounces lager

Pour the tomato juice into the beer. You can embellish it with a lemon slice if you desire.

Red-Headed Stepchild

14 ounces light beer   ½ ounce grenadine
1 ounce whiskey

Pour all ingredients into a glass. Gently mix.

Ruby

15 ounces Guinness stout   dash nutmeg
1 ounce ruby port

Pour the ruby port into the Guinness stout. Sprinkle with nutmeg.

Sake Bomb

1 ounce sake   15 ounces Zima

Pour the sake into a shot glass and the Zima into a pint glass. Drop the shot glass into the Zima. For a fun variation, balance the shot of sake over the Zima with a pair of chopsticks. Slam the table to make the shot fall into the Zima and drink. You can also substitute a light beer for the Zima.

Shandy

8 ounces Sprite or 7-Up   8 ounces light beer

Start with both ingredients chilled. In a beer glass, mix Sprite or 7-Up with the beer.

Skip and Go Naked

10 ounces light beer   5 ounces limeade
1 ounce gin

Combine the beer, gin, and limeade. Stir gently to mix.

Skippy

2 ounces vodka
6 ounces lemonade
8 ounces lager

Pour the vodka and lemonade into a glass. Fill with the lager.

Snake in the Apple Tree

8 ounces stout
8 ounces apple cider

Start with both ingredients chilled. Mix the stout and apple cider in a beer glass.

Sneaky Pete

15 ounces light beer
1 ounce applejack

Pour beer into a chilled mug and add applejack. Stir slightly.

South Wind

15 ounces light beer
1 ounce melon liqueur

Pour the melon liqueur into the beer. Stir gently to mix thoroughly until a pretty green.

Spiced Beer

12 ounces light beer
2 ounces ginger ale
¼ ounce simple syrup
¼ teaspoon ground ginger
pinch nutmeg
dash bitters

Pour the beer and ginger ale into a glass. Add the simple syrup, ginger, nutmeg, and bitters.

Sugar and Spice and Everything Nice

bottle or can Guinness Stout
¼ cup sweetened condensed milk
pinch of cinnamon
pinch of nutmeg
1 packet cocoa mix

Pour the chilled Guinness stout beer into a bowl. Add chilled condensed milk, cinnamon, nutmeg, and cocoa mix and stir until blended. Pour into a tall beer glass and enjoy.

Tomahawk

8 ounces stout
1 ounce vodka
7 ounces Smirnoff Ice

Pour the vodka into the stout. Fill with Smirnoff Ice.

Beer Trivia

In 1490, Columbus found Native Americans making beer from corn and black birch sap. In 1876, Louis Pasteur learned the secrets of yeast in the fermentation process and also learned to pasteurize beer twenty-two years before the same was done to milk. In 1909, Teddy Roosevelt took 500 gallons of beer on safari in Africa. In 1963, the stainless steel beer keg was introduced.

Tropical Beer

11 ounces light beer
1 ounce lemon-flavored rum
¼ ounce peach schnapps

3 ounces ginger ale
½ ounce lime juice cordial
½ ounce grenadine

Pour all ingredients into a tall glass in the order given. Stir once, gently.

Whistle Belly

1 ounce dark rum
1 ounce molasses

14 ounces ale

Pour the rum and molasses into the beer and gently mix.

Chapter 4

Wine, Champagne, Cognac, and Brandy

Wine is a fermented beverage made from fruits—and not necessarily grapes. Wine is most definitely a blast from the past. The first written account of it is in the Bible, which tells us that Noah planted a vineyard and made wine. Before that, wine was probably discovered by accident due to grape spoilage. Researchers say that social wine drinking probably began around 6000 BCE. In some cultures beer was for the villagers and workers, but wine was reserved for royalty. The Romans are truly responsible for expanding the wine culture in the Old World, mainly due to the sheer size of the Roman Empire.

Through the Grapevine

There are four types of wine: still, aromatized, sparkling, and fortified. Aromatized and fortified wines are described in the chapter on aperitifs, and sparkling refers to the champagne in this chapter. Still wines are the familiar red and white varieties that range in taste from dry and semidry to sweet.

Choosing Wine

Facing the forest of wine bottles at the liquor or grocery store can be daunting. The following list describes wines in the most general way with the barest descriptions. The best way to learn about wine is to investigate and experiment yourself. Individual taste is the best standard for personal pleasure. White wines are served chilled and red wines are served at room temperature. Also, the name of a wine clues you in to the type of grapes used. For example, a Cabernet Sauvignon is made from Cabernet Sauvignon grapes.

Popular Wines

Popular red wines include Cabernet Sauvignon (full bodied and dark), Merlot (medium bodied and lighter than Cabernet), Burgundy (heavy and dark) Beaujolais (light bodied and tastes better chilled), Pinot Noir (light bodied and mild), Zinfandel (medium bodied and spicy), Petit Syrah (rich berry flavor), and Chianti (soft and smooth).

Popular white wines include Chardonnay (dry and crisp), Sauvignon Blanc (dry and citrusy), Chenin Blanc (fruity), Chablis (light and woody), Riesling (fruity and sweet), and Gewürztraminer (spicy sweet).

Bishop

2 ounces orange juice
1 ounce lemon juice
1 teaspoon sugar
4 ounces red wine

Pour juices and sugar into a mixing glass nearly filled with ice. Strain into a highball glass over ice. Fill with red wine.

Cardinal

1 ounce crème de cassis
red wine to fill

Fill half of a wine glass with ice. Add the crème de cassis. Fill with red wine.

Glogg

7 ounces red wine
½ ounce fresh lemon juice
1 teaspoon sugar
1 cinnamon stick

Warm up the first three ingredients on the stove or in a microwave. Pour into a mug or Irish coffee glass. Garnish with a cinnamon stick.

Kir

½ ounce crème de cassis (or to taste)
4 ounces dry white wine
lemon twist

Pour the cassis into a large wine glass. Add the wine. Serve with a lemon twist.

Mulled Wine

orange zest from a quarter of an orange
lemon zest from a quarter of a lemon
1 tablespoon sugar
1 cinnamon stick
2 whole cloves
4 ounces water
5 ounces red wine
orange slices from a quarter of an orange
lemon slices from a quarter of a lemon

Put the fruit zest, sugar, cinnamon stick, cloves, and water into a small pot and bring to a slow boil. Remove from heat and add the wine. Add the orange and lemon slices and warm on low heat for 40 minutes (do NOT boil). Strain and serve.

Sangria #1

4 ounces red wine
1 ounce blackberry brandy
½ ounce orange juice
½ ounce pineapple juice
soda water or Perrier to fill
sliced seasonal fruits

Fill a tall glass or large wine glass with ice and add the first four ingredients. Fill with soda, leaving one inch from the rim. Garnish with slices of seasonal fruits.

Valentine

4 ounces Beaujolais
2 ounces cranberry juice

Combine ingredients in a shaker half filled with ice. Shake, then strain into a wine glass.

Vino Crush

4 ounces white wine   orange soda to fill
1 ounce Grand Marnier

Fill a tall glass with ice and pour in the wine and Grand Marnier. Fill with the orange soda.

White or Red Wine Cooler

5 ounces wine
Sprite or 7-Up to fill
lemon or lime wedge

Pour wine and soda over ice into a large wine glass. Stir gently. Garnish with a fruit wedge.

Wine Words to Know

Aging = Effects of maturation. Alcoholic fermentation = The process by which yeast and sugar in grapes react to produce alcohol. AC = Appellation d'Origine Contrôlée, the quality control designation on French wine. Claret = English term for red wine. Demi-Sec = Medium sweet. Doux = Sweet. Fortified wine = Wine with a high-strength spirit added.

White or Red Wine Spritzer

5 ounces red or white wine
club soda or sparkling water to fill
lemon or lime wedge

Pour wine and soda over ice into a large wine glass. Stir gently. Garnish with a fruit wedge.

White Sangria #1

4 ounces white wine
½ ounce apple brandy
1 ounce apple juice

¼ teaspoon ground cinnamon
soda water or Perrier to fill
sliced seasonal fruits

Fill a tall glass or large wine glass with ice and add the first four ingredients. Fill with soda, leaving one inch from the rim. Garnish with slices of seasonal fruits.

A Touch of Bubbly: Champagne

Champagne is sexy, no doubt about it. Its bubbles are flirtatious, and its fizz is a sultry invitation to hold hands, sigh, and exchange glances. "Champagne" is a term often used to describe any sparkling wine, but that is technically incorrect. Genuine champagne is only produced in France, in the chalky hills and valleys near the River Marne that make up the Champagne region. But the champagne method (*méthode champenoise*) of fermenting wine in the bottle it is sold in can be used anywhere to make still wine sparkle.

The method to make champagne begins with a cuvée, a vineyard's blend of dry white wines. The blend is bottled with yeast and sugar for a second fermentation to create the bubbles. In the process a sediment is formed. *Mon Dieu!* No matter how fine the wine, gunk in the bottle will not do. So the second step ingeniously collects the sediment. The bottles are tilted and turned so that the sediment clings to the cork. In the third step, the cork (along with the unsightly muck) is removed, a bit of sugar is added, and the bottle is recorked. The typical mushroom-shaped cork is a result of ramming two-thirds of a cork wider than the neck into the bottle. Under pressure, the cork forms a perfect seal. The wire on top is to prevent any over exuberant bubbles from popping their cork.

A champagne bottle should be opened with the same caution used in handling a dangerous weapon. Imagine the bottle as a gun and your finger as the safety catch. Always keep a thumb or finger over the cork. First remove the foil and wire, with your thumb hovering over the cork. Then point the bottle at a 45-degree angle away from everybody. Grip the cork firmly in one hand and pull with the other. As the internal pressure loosens the cork, continue to hold it firmly.

Champagne offers choices but also clear descriptions. Created in a range from dry to sweet, the contents of the bottles are conveniently labeled. Brut is very dry; extra dry or sec is not as dry; demi-sec is the half-and-half of champagne, slightly sweet and dry; and doux is the sweetest of all.

🍸 Bellini

1 ounce chilled white peach purée
Prosecco sparkling wine to fill

Pour the purée into a champagne flute and fill with Prosecco. You can buy the purée or hand-make some. A lot of people use champagne and a peach nectar or liqueur, but this recipe stays true to the original 1948 concoction.

♷ Black Velvet

6 ounces chilled champagne or sparkling wine
6 ounces stout or dark porter

Simply float the chilled stout on top of chilled champagne. Do not stir. Created in honor of Queen Victoria's husband, Prince Albert, after his death in 1861.

Champagne and Chambord

1 ounce Chambord (high-end raspberry liqueur)
chilled champagne to fill

Pour the Chambord into a champagne flute and fill with champagne.

Champagne Antoine

1 ounce gin
1 ounce dry vermouth
⅛ ounce Pernod

chilled dry champagne to fill
lemon twist

Shake the gin, vermouth, and Pernod with ice. Strain into a champagne flute. Fill with champagne and add a lemon twist.

Wine Words to Know

Jug wine = American term for table wine. Sec = Dry. Tannin = Natural component in skins, seeds, and stems of grapes that creates a dry, puckering sensation in the mouth. Varietal = Grape variety; wines made from a single grape are "varietals," and labeled with that grape. Vintage = Defines the grape harvest of a single year.

Y Champagne Cocktail

6 ounces champagne, chilled   3 dashes angostura bitters
1 sugar cube   lemon twist

Pour a glass of champagne. Soak a cube of sugar with the bitters. Drop cube into the champagne and add the twist.

Champagne Fizz or Diamond Fizz

2 ounces gin   1 teaspoon sugar
1 ounce lemon juice   chilled champagne to fill

Combine gin, lemon juice, and sugar in a shaker half filled with ice and shake. Strain into a highball glass over ice. Fill with champagne.

Champagne Flamingo

¾ ounce vodka   chilled champagne to fill
¾ ounce Campari   zest of orange

Shake vodka and Campari with ice and strain into a champagne flute. Fill with champagne. Garnish with a zest of orange.

Champagne Mint

½ ounce green crème de menthe   chilled champagne to fill

Pour crème de menthe into a flute and fill with champagne.

Death in the Afternoon

1 ounce Pernod (or other absinthe substitute)
chilled champagne to fill

Pour Pernod into a champagne flute. Fill with champagne.

> **Bubbly Bath**
> Rumor has it that Marilyn Monroe once filled up her tub with 350 bottles of champagne and took a bath.

Flirtini

½ ounce pineapple vodka   champagne to fill
1 ounce pineapple juice

Shake the vodka and pineapple juice. Strain into a champagne flute. Fill with champagne.

French 75

1 ounce gin   champagne to fill
1 ounce lemon juice   lemon twist
½ ounce simple syrup

Build into a champagne flute and top with chilled champagne. Garnish with a lemon twist.

Kir Royale

1 ounce crème de cassis   lemon twist
chilled champagne to fill

Pour the crème de cassis into a champagne flute and fill with champagne. Garnish with a lemon twist.

Melon Mimosa

1 ounce melon liqueur   5 ounces champagne, chilled
1 teaspoon lime cordial

Combine ingredients in a champagne flute or white wine glass. Stir gently.

∇ Mimosa

¼ of a champagne flute of freshly squeezed orange juice
champagne to fill
strawberry

Fill a champagne flute a quarter of the way with orange juice.
Fill with champagne and garnish the rim with a strawberry.

Serving Champagne

Keep the cork pointed away from anything it could hurt
or break if it accidentally comes out (at 100 miles per
hour!). Release the cork by turning the bottle, not the
cork. You should hear a soft hiss and pop. To pour, hold
the bottom of the bottle with your thumb into the punt
(the dent in the bottom of the bottle) and your fingers
spread underneath.

Pimm's Royale

¼ ounce Pimm's Cup
chilled champagne to fill
cucumber spear

Pour the Pimm's Cup in a champagne flute. Fill with chilled
champagne and garnish with a cucumber spear.

Poinsettia

½ ounce cranberry juice   chilled champagne to fill
¼ ounce triple sec   lime twist

Pour the juice and the triple sec in a champagne flute. Fill with
chilled champagne and garnish with a twist of lime.

Cognac and Brandy

Cognac and brandy are distilled wines. All cognacs are brandy, but not all brandies are cognacs. Brandy can be made from any fruit (including grapes). Cognac must be made in the Cognac region of France from grapes grown in the same place. Cognacs are distilled twice and stored in oak casks made from the wood of the trees grown in the Cognac region. The length of the aging process varies and distillers offer a guide for the buyer. There are three general classifications to separate cognacs from each other—VS ("very special," aged at least two years), VSOP ("very superior old pale," aged at least four years), and XO ("extra old," aged at least six years).

Aside from cognac, there are many types of brandies. The vintners of California distill brandies from their own grapes, which tend to be lighter and smoother. There is a dry Italian brandy called grappa; apple brandies such as calvados; kirschwasser, or kirsch, made from cherries; poire Williams, made from pears; framboise, made from raspberries; fraise, made from strawberries; and slivovitz, made from plums. These are true brandies, distilled directly from fruits. Other fruit-flavored "brandies" may actually be liqueurs created from a variety of liquors. They are not necessarily inferior, just not made directly from fruit or grape wine.

Ambrosia

1 ounce applejack	juice of ½ lemon
1 ounce brandy	chilled champagne to fill
dash triple sec	

Pour the first four ingredients into an ice-filled shaker. Shake well and strain into a highball glass over ice. Fill with champagne and stir gently.

Apricot Sour

2 ounces apricot brandy
3 ounces sour mix
1 cherry

Pour the brandy and sour mix into a shaker tin of ice. Shake and strain over a highball glass of ice. Garnish with a cherry.

B&B

1 ounce Bénédictine
1 ounce brandy

Pour the Bénédictine and the brandy into a brandy snifter.

Baby Doll

2 ounces cognac   juice of half a lemon
1½ ounces Grand Marnier   sugar for rimming

Pour the cognac, Grand Marnier, and lemon juice into a shaker tin of ice. Shake and strain into a sugar-rimmed cocktail glass.

Beautiful

1 ounce cognac
1 ounce Grand Marnier

Pour ingredients into a brandy snifter and serve.

Between the Sheets

¾ ounce light rum
¾ ounce brandy
¾ ounce triple sec

½ ounce lemon juice
lemon twist

Pour all ingredients into shaker. Shake with ice. Strain into a martini glass. Garnish with a lemon twist.

Bombay Cocktail

1 ounce brandy
½ ounce dry vermouth
½ ounce triple sec

½ ounce sweet vermouth
lemon twist

Pour liquid ingredients into a cocktail shaker nearly filled with ice. Shake, then strain into a cocktail glass. Garnish with a lemon twist.

Brandy Alexander

1½ ounces brandy
1 ounce dark crème de cacao

1 ounce cream or half-and-half
sprinkle of nutmeg

Combine first three ingredients in a shaker nearly filled with ice. Shake, then strain into a cocktail glass. Sprinkle with nutmeg. This cocktail can also be prepared in the blender.

Brandy Cassis

1½ ounces brandy
¼ ounce crème de cassis
1 ounce lemon juice
lemon twist

Combine liquid ingredients in a shaker nearly filled with ice.
Strain into a cocktail glass. Serve with a lemon twist.

Brandy Manhattan

1½ ounces brandy
1 ounce sweet vermouth
1 teaspoon sugar
dash bitters

Pour all ingredients into a shaker of ice and shake. Strain into
a cocktail glass.

Brandy Milk Punch

1 ounce brandy
4 ounces whole milk
1 teaspoon powdered sugar
1 teaspoon vanilla extract

Combine the ingredients in a cocktail shaker with ice. Shake
and strain into a highball glass filled with crushed ice.

Brandy Vermouth Classic

2 ounces brandy
½ ounce sweet vermouth
dash bitters

Combine ingredients in a mixing glass half filled with ice and
stir. Strain into a cocktail glass.

Calvados Cocktail

1½ ounces calvados apple brandy
2 ounces orange juice
orange twist

Combine liquid ingredients in a shaker filled with ice. Shake;
then strain into a cocktail glass. Serve with an orange twist.

Combustible Edison

1 ounce Campari
1 ounce fresh lemon juice
2 ounces brandy

Shake the Campari and lemon juice with ice and strain into a
cocktail glass, leaving an inch from the rim. Pour the brandy
in a snifter and heat it for 10 seconds in the microwave. Light
the brandy with a match, then pour the flaming stream into
the cocktail glass.

Creamy Mocha Alexander

1 ounce brandy
1 ounce coffee liqueur
1 ounce dark crème de cacao
2 scoops of ice cream

Put all ingredients into a blender and blend without ice. Pour
into a tall glass.

Napoleon

Napoleon loved cognac. As a matter of fact, he made
the Courvoisier distillery his headquarters during the
French Revolution. Today, Courvoisier makes a Napoleon cognac as a tribute.

Delovely

1 ounce brandy
1 ounce calvados
¼ ounce lemon juice
¼ ounce grenadine

Shake the ingredients with ice in a cocktail shaker. Strain into a cocktail glass.

Dirty Mother

1 ounce brandy
1 ounce coffee liqueur

Build the ingredients in a rocks glass of ice.

Dirty White Mother

1 ounce brandy
2 ounces cream or half-and-half
1 ounce coffee liqueur

Shake the ingredients with ice in a cocktail shaker. Strain into a highball glass of ice.

Dream Cocktail

2 ounces brandy
1 teaspoon anisette
½ ounce triple sec

Combine ingredients in a shaker nearly filled with ice. Shake and strain into a cocktail glass.

Fancy Brandy

2 ounces brandy
¼ ounce Cointreau
¼ teaspoon sugar

dash bitters
lemon twist

Pour liquid ingredients into a mixing glass nearly filled with ice and stir. Strain into a cocktail glass. Serve with a lemon twist.

French Passion

1 ounce cognac   1 ounce Alizé Red Passion liqueur

Build in a rocks glass of ice.

Jack Rose

1½ ounces apple brandy   ½ ounce grenadine
1 ounce fresh lime juice

Combine ingredients in a shaker nearly filled with ice. Shake and strain into a cocktail glass.

Kama Sutra Martini

1 ounce Alizé   1 ounce orange juice
1 ounce Alizé Red Passion liqueur

Shake well with ice and strain into a martini glass.

Alizé

Alizé (al-la-ZAY) is a blend of cognac and passion fruit. Even though it first hit the market in 1986, it wasn't until Tupac Shakur mentioned a drink named "Thug Passion" in a 1990s rap song that it skyrocketed to fame among the hip-hop generation.

Keoke Coffee (also called Coffee Nudge)

½ ounce brandy
½ ounce coffee liqueur

hot black coffee to fill

Pour the ingredients into a mug or Irish coffee mug.

Rimmed Brothers Grimm Cocoa

1 teaspoon sugar
½ teaspoon cinnamon powder
1 ounce Irish cream

1 packet hot cocoa
hot water to fill
whipped cream or miniature
marshmallows (optional)

Mix the sugar and cinnamon together on a saucer. Wet the rim of a mug and dip it in the cinnamon-sugar mix. Pour the Irish cream and the cocoa into the mug. Fill with hot water and stir. Garnish with whipped cream or mini marshmallows.

Separator

1 ounce brandy
1 ounce coffee liqueur

2 ounces cream or
half-and-half

Build in a rocks glass of ice.

Y Sidecar

2 ounces brandy
½ ounce Cointreau
1 ounce fresh lemon juice

Combine ingredients in a shaker nearly filled with ice. Shake and strain into a cocktail glass.

Sonata

1 ounce cognac
1 ounce amaretto

Pour both ingredients into a brandy snifter.

Y Stinger

1 ounce brandy
¼ ounce white crème de menthe

Build in a rocks glass of ice.

Chapter 5

Aperitifs, Cordials, and Liqueurs

An aperitif (uh-pair-a-TEEF) is an alcoholic drink taken before dinner. Aperitifs are meant to stimulate your appetite. Cordials and liqueurs are often used as after-dinner drinks to aid digestion.

Aperitifs and Nightcaps

Leisurely get-togethers allow guests to savor their conversation and their drinks while they wait for their meal. Aperitifs include sherry, port, vermouths, Lillet, Dubonnet, Becherovka, and cocktails made with Campari, pastis, ouzo, and Cynar. The first five mentioned are wine-based but were not talked about in the preceding wine chapter because they are more pertinent to this chapter.

After-dinner drinks often help with digestion. Europeans drink shots of limoncello, minted schnapps, grappa, and anise liqueurs. Today, after-dinner drinks tend to be either creamy, hot, or a neat measure of spirit. Nightcaps can be a hot drink or a single spirit that is sipped to make you feel warm and cozy inside. If you like the taste of anise/licorice (pastis), there are many other choices for you—Galliano, anisette, ouzo, sambuca, pastis, Ricard, Pernod, or other absinthe substitute.

Absinthe (AB-sinth) has an intriguing history. Absinthe originated in Switzerland and legend says that the inventor was Dr. Pierre Ordinaire. It was one of the original ingredients in the first cocktail, the Sazerac. But absinthe also had a darker, more dangerous side. This pastis had a high alcohol content and was made with wormwood, which caused slight hallucinations, earning it the nickname the Green Fairy (*La Fée Verte*).

By 1898, absinthe was banned in Brazil. Other countries followed—Belgium in 1906, Holland in 1908, Switzerland in 1910, and the United States and France in 1912. It was eventually outlawed in many parts of Europe and

North America. Recently, due to relegalization in most of Europe, producers use clever marketing, extravagant claims, and flashy and hip labels to sell less-than-worthy imitations. There is one hope—a New Orleans absinthe historian, chemist, and environmental microbiologist named T. A. Breaux. Breaux has cracked the absinthe code, recreating the absinthe one could have found over 100 years ago and selling his concoction where it is legal. Speaking of which, absinthe *isn't* legal in the United States. Absinthe substitutes on the market are usually made with anise and popular products include Pernod and Herbsaint.

Aperitif, Cordial, and Liqueur Recipes

Adirondack Mint

1 ounce Godiva chocolate liqueur
1 ounce peppermint schnapps
5 ounces hot chocolate
whipped cream

Pour all ingredients into an Irish coffee glass or mug and stir. Top with whipped cream.

Affair

1 ounce strawberry schnapps
1 ounce cranberry juice
1 ounce orange juice

Pour all ingredients into an ice-filled mixing glass. Stir well, then strain into a cocktail glass.

After Five

1 ounce Irish cream liqueur
1 ounce Kahlúa
1 ounce peppermint schnapps

Pour all ingredients into an ice-filled rocks glass. Stir gently.

Afternoon Delight

1 ounce banana liqueur
1 ounce white crème de cacao
1 scoop banana ice cream
1 scoop chocolate ice cream

Put all ingredients into a blender and blend. For a creamier drink, add cream or milk little by little while the blender is on. Pour into a tall glass.

Liqueur Brands

There are many liqueur brands on the market, but the top four that make crèmes, schnapps, cordials, and liqueurs are DeKuyper, Bols, Marie Brizard, and Hiram Walker.

Almond Joy

1 ounce Coco Lopez   1 ounce crème de cacao
1 ounce amaretto   2 ounces half-and-half

Pour ingredients into a shaker with ice. Shake, then strain into a highball glass of ice.

♼ Americano

1 ounce Campari
1 ounce sweet vermouth

Pour Campari and sweet vermouth into rocks glass filled with ice and stir.

The Americano
It's said that the Americano was created by Italian Gaspare Campari at his bar, Café Campari, in the 1860s. It used to have another name, but Gaspare noticed that the American tourists love the drink so he renamed it.

Armagnac Lillet

2 ounces Lillet Blanc
2 ounces Armagnac
orange wedge

Pour Lillet Blanc and Armagnac over crushed ice in a champagne glass. Garnish with an orange wedge.

♼ Banshee

1 ounce banana liqueur
1 ounce white crème de cacao
2 ounces cream

Combine ingredients in a shaker. Shake, then pour into a cocktail glass.

Baronial

2 ounces Lillet Blanc
1 ounce gin
¼ ounce Cointreau
dash bitters

Pour all ingredients into an ice-filled mixing glass. Stir well, then strain into a cocktail glass.

Black Honey

1½ ounces Drambuie
hot coffee to fill
1 tablespoon honey
whipped cream (optional)

Pour the Drambuie into a coffee mug and fill with coffee. Add the honey and stir to dissolve. Top with whipped cream if you desire.

History of Drambuie

On every Drambuie bottle you'll find its story. In 1746, Prince Charles Edward Stuart gave Captain John Mackinnon the recipe in appreciation for taking care of him during the prince's (unsuccessful) bid for the British throne. The word is Gaelic for "the drink that satisfies."

 ## Black Russian

1 ounce Kahlúa   1 ounce vodka

Build in a short glass of ice.

Bittersweet Cocktail

1 ounce sweet vermouth   lemon twist
1 ounce dry vermouth

Pour liquid ingredients into a mixing glass nearly filled with ice and stir. Strain into a cocktail glass. Add a lemon twist.

Butterscotch Coffee

1 ounce butterscotch schnapps   hot coffee to fill
½ ounce Frangelico   ½ ounce hazelnut creamer

Pour the schnapps and the Frangelico into a coffee mug. Fill with coffee. Add the hazelnut creamer and stir.

Caramel Appletini

1 ounce sour apple schnapps   1 ounce butterscotch schnapps
1 ounce apple-flavored vodka

Pour all ingredients into a shaker tin of ice. Shake, then strain into a cocktail glass.

Flavors of Liqueurs

Absinthe = anise/licorice; advocaat = eggnog; amaretto = almond; anisette = anise/licorice; aquavit = caraway; Bailey's Irish cream = vanilla, chocolate, and Irish whiskey; Bärenjäger = honey; Bénédictine = herbs and spices; blue curaçao = orange; Chambord = black raspberry; Chartreuse = herbs and spices; Cherry Heering: cherry; coffee liqueur = coffee and chocolate.

Charming Proposal

1 ounce sour apple schnapps
1 ounce passion liqueur

¼ ounce grenadine
ginger ale to fill

Pour the first three ingredients into a tall glass of ice. Stir, then fill with the ginger ale.

Chocolate Monkey

1 ounce coffee liqueur
1 ounce crème de banana
1 ounce chocolate syrup

5 ounces cream
1 banana

Blend all ingredients with a cup of ice.

Colorado Bulldog

1 ounce coffee liqueur
1 ounce vodka

2 ounces cream
cola to fill

Pour coffee liqueur, vodka, and cream into a shaker. Shake, then pour into a highball glass of ice and fill with cola.

Come Hither

1 ounce vodka
1 ounce white crème de cacao

½ ounce Galliano
2 ounces cream

Pour vodka, white crème de cacao, Galliano, and cream into a shaker tin of ice. Shake and strain into a cocktail glass.

Coronation

3 ounces dry sherry
½ ounce dry vermouth

dash bitters
lemon twist

Combine liquids in a shaker half filled with ice. Shake well. Strain into a cocktail glass and garnish with lemon twist.

Cortés

1 ounce Kahlúa   dash lemon juice
1 ounce light rum

Combine and serve over cracked ice in a brandy snifter.

Diablo Cocktail

1 ounce brandy
1 ounce dry vermouth
1 ounce Cointreau
dash angostura bitters
dash Regans' orange bitters

Combine ingredients in a shaker half filled with ice. Shake well. Strain into a cocktail glass.

Dry Negroni

1 ounce Campari   1 ounce gin
1 ounce dry vermouth

Pour ingredients into an old-fashioned glass over ice. Stir gently.

Flavors of Liqueurs

Kahlúa = chocolate coffee; Lichido = litchi; Licor 43 = citrus vanilla; limoncello = sweet lemon; Malibu = coconut; manzana = apple; Midori = honeydew melon; Parfait Amour = violets, rose, vanilla, and spice; Passoã = passion fruit; patxaran = sloe berry, coffee bean, and vanilla; Pernod = anise/licorice; Pisang Ambon = banana; prunelle = plum.

Dubonnet Cocktail

1 ounce Dubonnet
1 ounce gin
lemon twist

Combine ingredients in a shaker half filled with ice. Shake well. Strain into a cocktail glass and garnish with lemon twist.

Dubonnet Rouge

2 ounces Dubonnet
1 ounce applejack
lemon twist

Combine ingredients in a shaker half filled with ice. Shake well. Strain into a cocktail glass and garnish with lemon twist.

Foreign Affair

2 ounces sambuca
1 ounce brandy

Pour both ingredients into a shaker tin of ice. Shake and strain into a cocktail glass.

Frog in a Blender

1 ounce coffee liqueur
1 ounce green crème de menthe
2 ounces cream
½ ounce red cinnamon schnapps

Put a cup of ice into a blender. Pour in the first three ingredients and blend. Pour into a tall glass and add the red cinnamon schnapps on top. This drink can also be shaken and strained into a cocktail glass.

Frozen Girl Scout Cookie

1 ounce dark crème de cacao
½ ounce Frangelico
½ ounce Irish cream
½ ounce butterscotch schnapps
¼ ounce cinnamon schnapps
2 scoops vanilla ice cream
whipped cream

Pour all ingredients except the whipped cream into a blender and blend. Pour into a tall glass and top with whipped cream.

Fuzzy Navel

2 ounces peach schnapps
orange juice to fill

Pour the peach schnapps into a highball glass of ice and fill to the top with orange juice.

Flavors of Liqueurs
Razzmatazz = raspberry; Rumple Minze = peppermint; sambuca = anise/licorice; sloe gin = sloe berry; Southern Comfort = peach, apricot, and honey; Strega = herbs, mint, fennel, and saffron; Tequila Rose = strawberry cream; Tia Maria = coffee; triple sec = orange; tsipouro = anise/licorice; Tuaca = caramel, vanilla, orange; Whidbeys = loganberry; xtabentun = anise/licorice; Yukon Jack = honey.

Godfather

1 ounce amaretto   1 ounce Scotch whiskey

Pour amaretto and whiskey into a rocks glass of ice. Sir gently.

 Godmother

1 ounce amaretto   1 ounce vodka

Pour amaretto and vodka into a rocks glass of ice. Sir gently.

 Golden Cadillac

1 ounce Galliano
1 ounce white crème de cacao
2 ounces cream

Pour all ingredients into a shaker. Shake, then pour into a cocktail glass.

Good Karma

1 ounce raspberry liqueur   1 ounce pineapple juice
1 ounce melon liqueur   1 ounce sweet-and-sour mix

Pour all ingredients into a shaker tin of ice and shake. Strain it into a cocktail glass.

Grasshopper

1 ounce green crème de menthe   2 ounces cream
1 ounce white crème de cacao

Pour the green crème de menthe, white crème de cacao, and cream into a shaker tin of ice. Shake and strain into a cocktail glass. This drink can also be served frozen and made with vanilla ice cream instead of cream.

Green-Eyed Blonde

1 ounce melon liqueur
1 ounce banana liqueur

1 ounce Irish cream
2 ounces cream or milk

Pour all ingredients into a shaker tin of ice. Shake and strain into a cocktail glass.

Sweetly Seductive

Served straight in its own glass, a liqueur is sweetly seductive. Indeed, with a 2.5 percent minimum sugar content, liqueurs are the dessert of drinks. Many are even sweeter, and the crèmes, whose creamy consistency stems from high sugar content, are the richest of all. But their sweetness never overwhelms their fruit or herb character, so all liqueurs will add intense, distinctive flavors to mixed drinks.

Honeymoon Suite

1 ounce Irish cream
1 ounce hazelnut liqueur
½ ounce coffee liqueur

½ ounce honey
2 ounces cream or milk
2 chocolate kisses

Pour all ingredients except the kisses into a shaker tin of ice. Shake and strain into a cocktail glass. Unwrap two chocolate kisses and drop them into the cocktail.

Love Potion

1 ounce Parfait Amour
1 ounce raspberry vodka
white (clear) cranberry juice and club soda to fill
sprig of purple seedless grapes

Pour Parfait Amour and vodka into a tall glass of ice. Fill with equal parts of white (clear) cranberry juice and club soda. Garnish with the grapes.

Lucky Charm

1 ounce Tequila Rose strawberry cream liqueur
1 ounce white crème de menthe
3 ounces milk
Lucky Charms cereal marshmallows

Pour the liquid ingredients into a shaker tin of ice and shake. Strain into a cocktail glass and add the Lucky Charms marshmallows on top.

Negroni

1 ounce gin   1 ounce Campari
1 ounce sweet vermouth   lemon twist

Pour ingredients into a shaker. Shake and strain into a rocks glass of ice. Garnish with a lemon twist.

Nuts and Berries

1 ounce Frangelico   cream or milk to fill
1 ounce Chambord

Pour the Frangelico and Chambord into a short glass of ice. Fill with cream or milk.

Nutty Irishman

1 ounce Frangelico
1 ounce Irish cream
cream or milk to fill

Pour the Frangelico and Irish cream into a short glass of ice.
Fill with cream or milk.

Orgasm

1 ounce coffee liqueur
1 ounce amaretto
2 ounces Irish cream (optional)

Pour ingredients into a shaker. Shake and pour into a short
glass of ice. Cream can be added if desired.

What Is Schnapps?

Schnapps is made from grains, fruit, or herbs fermented
and distilled together. Liqueurs are made by steeping
herbs and fruits in an alcohol that had already been fermented and distilled. This is the reason schnapps can
have a high alcohol content.

Peppermint Pattie

1 ounce dark crème de cacao   2 ounces cream (optional)
1 ounce white crème de menthe

Pour the ingredients in a short glass of ice. Cream can be
added if desired.

Picon Fizz

½ ounce Amer Picon
½ ounce cognac or brandy

¼ ounce grenadine
club soda to fill

Pour the first three ingredients into a highball glass of ice. Fill with club soda.

Pimm's Cup

1½ ounces Pimm's No. 1
club soda to fill

lemon wedge
cucumber slice

Pour the Pimm's into a highball glass of ice. Fill with club soda. Garnish with a lemon wedge and slice of cucumber.

Pink Squirrel

1 ounce crème de noyaux
1 ounce white crème de cacao

2 ounces cream

Shake all ingredients in a shaker tin half filled with ice. Pour into a cocktail glass.

Platinum Blonde Coffee

1½ ounces Godiva white chocolate liqueur
hot black coffee to fill
whipped cream (optional)

Pour the Godiva white chocolate liqueur into a coffee mug and fill with coffee. Garnish with whipped cream if desired.

Queen Elizabeth

1 ounce Bénédictine

2 ounces sweet vermouth

Pour both ingredients into a shaker tin of ice and shake. Strain into a cocktail glass.

Root Beer Float

1 ounce Galliano
1 ounce vanilla schnapps
1 ounce cream

root beer to fill
whipped cream

Fill a tall glass with ice and pour Galliano, schnapps, and cream. Fill with root beer and garnish with whipped cream.

Ruby Sipper

1½ ounces DeKuyper's Hot Damn cinnamon schnapps
hot apple cider to fill

Pour the cinnamon schnapps into a coffee mug. Fill with hot apple cider.

Sambuca

2 ounces sambuca
3 coffee beans

Pour sambuca into a brandy snifter or cordial glass. Add coffee beans.

Coffee Beans
Sambuca gets three coffee beans when served to savor. You can leave them out if you are serving it for shots. The beans are good luck and mean many things to many people. The most popular meanings are health, happiness, and prosperity.

Scarlett O'Hara

2 ounces Southern Comfort
3 ounces cranberry juice

Build in a short glass of ice and stir.

Smith & Kearns

2 ounces coffee liqueur
2 ounces cream
club soda to fill

Pour coffee liqueur and cream into a shaker. Shake and pour into a highball glass of ice. Top with club soda.

Smith & Wesson

1 ounce coffee liqueur   2 ounces half-and-half
1 ounce vodka   club soda to fill

Pour the first three ingredients into a highball glass of ice. Top with club soda.

Sombrero

2 ounces Kahlúa
2 ounces cream

Build in a short glass of ice. Serve layered.

Southern Hospitality

2 ounces Southern Comfort
2 ounces peach schnapps

Fill a shaker tin with ice and add the Southern Comfort and peach schnapps. Shake for about 20 seconds. Strain into a cocktail glass.

Sweet Vermouth on the Rocks

2 ounces sweet vermouth
lemon twist

Pour over ice in a short glass. Add a lemon twist.

Vermouth
Vermouth is a fortified wine flavored with herbs, spices, barks, and flowers. The flavors can be added through infusion, maceration, or distillation. There are many brands of vermouth produced in both Italy and France.

Toasted Almond

1 ounce coffee liqueur
1 ounce amaretto
2 ounces cream

Shake ingredients together. Pour into a short glass of ice.

Tootsie Roll

1 ounce coffee liqueur
1 ounce dark crème de cacao
3 ounces orange juice

Pour all ingredients into a shaker tin of ice. Shake and strain into a cocktail glass or pour over a short glass of ice.

Vermouth Cassis

2 ounces dry vermouth
1 ounce crème de cassis
club soda to fill

Combine vermouth and crème de cassis in a highball glass filled with ice. Fill with club soda.

Crème vs. Cream

A cream liqueur is not to be confused with a crème liqueur. If it says cream, it includes dairy cream. The best example is Bailey's Irish Cream. Crèmes have a lot of sugar added, giving them a syrup-like consistency. Crème refers to the consistency. Examples are crème de cacao, crème de menthe, and crème de banana.

White Caramel Apple Cider

1 ounce Dooley's toffee liqueur
½ ounce Tuaca
hot apple cider to fill
whipped cream (optional)

Pour the Dooley's toffee liqueur and Tuaca into a coffee mug. Fill with hot apple cider. Top with whipped cream if you desire.

White Russian

1 ounce Kahlúa
1 ounce vodka
2 ounces cream

Shake all ingredients and pour into a short glass of ice.

Chapter 6

Vodka: The Spirited Neutral

Milk comes from cows, wool comes from sheep, and vodka comes from potatoes. Not so fast. Yes, some vodka is made from potatoes. But unlike many spirits, vodka can be made anywhere in the world with practically anything that contains sugar or starch. Common ingredients (aside from potatoes, of course) include beets and grains such as corn and rye.

Vodka History

Legend tells us that in the 1300s, Genoese merchants en route to Lithuania brought this "water of life" (aqua vitae) to Moscow. Other sources contend that vodka originated in Poland and Russia without any assistance from the Genoese. By the 1700s, people were infusing vodka with herb and fruit flavors like sage, cherry, dill, blackberry, and caraway. (And we thought our modern society created flavored vodka!) Vodka didn't make it into American liquor cabinets until the 1930s—and the brand was Smirnoff. The classic cocktail Moscow Mule became popular in the 1950s despite its association with the menacing Communists on the other side of the Iron Curtain. In 1962, the first James Bond film showed 007 ordering a Martini made with Smirnoff, and vodka skyrocketed straight to the top. It has remained the number-one spirit in America since.

Vodka is a profound silent partner. Because it is chameleon-like, taking on the tastes of anything around it, flavored versions have flourished since the turn of the twenty-first century. New high-end vodkas are constantly produced with their own little gimmicks—vodka made with ice harvested from icebergs, black-colored vodka, vodka filtered multiple times, vodka infused with rose petals, vodka distilled from organic grains. . . The list goes on. Unfortunately, vodka's smooth taste makes it the number-one training-wheel spirit. Inexperienced drinkers tend to learn the hard way that tasteless does not equal painless. As always, moderation is the key to enjoying your "white whiskey."

Barmarche Honey Sour

1½ ounces Belvedere vodka
1½ ounces honey
¼ ounce B&B
1 ounce lemon juice

half an egg white
dash bitters
orange and cherry flag

Stir together the vodka and honey to start this award-winning cocktail. Stir in the rest of the ingredients. Shake and strain into a rocks glass of fresh ice or into a cocktail glass. Garnish with an orange and cherry flag. Invented by Clark Clark of the Barmarche Bar in New York City.

Baybreeze

1½ ounces vodka
pineapple and cranberry juice to fill

Pour all ingredients into a highball glass of ice.

Berry Bordello

1 ounce strawberry vodka
½ ounce raspberry vodka
½ ounce raspberry liqueur
cranberry juice to fill
berries

Pour the first three ingredients into a tall glass of ice. Fill with cranberry juice and stir. Garnish with berries.

Black Goose

1 ounce Grey Goose vodka
1 ounce coffee liqueur

Pour the Grey Goose vodka and coffee liqueur into a short glass of ice and stir.

Black Magic

2 ounces Blavod black vodka   7-Up to fill
½ ounce grenadine   maraschino cherry

Pour vodka and grenadine into a tall glass of ice. Fill with
7-Up and stir. Garnish with a maraschino cherry.

Black Martini

1 ounce Blavod black vodka   1 ounce triple sec
1 ounce raspberry liqueur   2 ounces sweet-and-sour mix

Pour all ingredients into a shaker tin of ice. Shake and strain
into a martini glass. This black drink looks nice with a white-
sugared rim.

Bloody Caesar

1½ shots vodka
¼ shot fresh lime juice
celery salt, pepper, Tabasco sauce, Worcestershire sauce to taste
Clamato juice (half tomato juice/half clam juice) to fill
celery

Combine all liquid ingredients and spices with ice and stir.
Strain into a tall glass filled with ice. Garnish with a stick of
celery.

Bloody Mary

2 ounces vodka
Bloody Mary mix to fill
celery stalk and lime wedge

Combine vodka and mix; stir with ice. Strain into a tall glass
filled with ice. Garnish with a stick of celery and lime wedge
and anything else your heart desires.

Bloody Mary History

Tomato juice followed quickly on the heels of the juicer, which was introduced in 1921. The Bloody Mary, a simple concoction of vodka and tomato juice, has disputed origins. Bartender Ferdinand Petiot claimed to have invented the drink in the late 1920s in Paris. Petiot took his drink to other bars, where it was renamed Bucket of Blood and Red Snapper, but the original name finally stuck. Another contender, George Jessel, said he mixed the drink for himself to cure a hangover. It is unknown who the Bloody Mary's namesake was, but the drink was not named for the Catholic Tudor queen who earned the grisly nickname after ordering Protestant purges.

Blue Lagoon

1 ounce raspberry vodka
1 ounce blue curaçao
Sprite to fill

Pour vodka and curaçao into a highball glass over ice. Fill with Sprite and stir.

Bull Shot

1½ ounces vodka
4 ounces chilled beef bouillon
dash Worcestershire sauce, salt, and pepper

Combine ingredients in a shaker half filled with ice. Shake well. Strain into a highball glass over ice.

Caipiroska

2 teaspoons sugar
half a lime   2 ounces vodka

Muddle the lime and sugar in a mixing glass. Add the vodka and ice. Shake, then strain into a rocks glass of cracked ice.

Cape Codder/Cape Cod

1 ounce vodka   lime wedge (optional)
cranberry juice to fill

Fill a highball glass with ice. Add the vodka. Fill with cranberry juice. Garnish with a lime wedge if desired.

The Cape Codder

The Cape Codder gets its name from the mixer used—cranberry juice. It refers to the cranberries that grow in the northeastern United States around Cape Cod in Massachusetts. In the fall, the berries turn a bright red color. Cranberries used for juice are harvested by flooding the fields so the berries float to the surface.

Chi-Chi

1½ ounces vodka
4 ounces piña colada mix
pineapple slice and cherry

Pour ingredients into a blender with a cup of ice. Blend. Pour into a tall glass of your choice. Garnish with pineapple slice and cherry.

Chiquita

1½ ounces vodka
½ ounce banana liqueur
¼ ounce amaretto
½ ounce lime juice
¼ cup sliced bananas

Combine ingredients in a blender with a cup of ice. Pour into a tall glass of your choice.

Chocolate Pudding Pop

1 ounce chocolate vodka
1 ounce coffee liqueur
1 ounce Irish cream

2 scoops chocolate ice cream
cream to blend
chocolate fudge pudding pop

Put the chocolate vodka, coffee liqueur, Irish cream, and ice cream in a blender. Blend, adding the cream little by little until a smooth consistency is achieved. Pour into a tall glass and garnish by sticking in a chocolate fudge pop.

Coconut Brownie with Nuts

1 ounce coconut rum
1 ounce vanilla vodka
1 ounce hazelnut liqueur
1 packet powdered hot chocolate

1 ounce Coco Lopez cream
1 scoop chocolate ice cream
1 scoop vanilla ice cream
1 ounce shredded coconut

Pour the coconut rum, vanilla vodka, hazelnut liqueur, chocolate and vanilla ice cream, powdered hot chocolate packet, and Coco Lopez into a blender. Blend. Add the cream little by little until drink reaches a smooth consistency. Pour into a tall glass and sprinkle shredded coconut on top.

Disaronno Amaretto

They say that in 1525, a church in Saronno, Italy, commissioned artist and Da Vinci student Bernardino Luini to paint its sanctuary with frescoes. Luini needed a model for the Madonna and chose the young widowed innkeeper. To show her gratitude, she steeped apricot kernels in brandy, which resulted in the liqueur Disaronno amaretto. Oh, they may have also been lovers.

Coconut Concubine

1 ounce coconut rum
1 ounce vanilla vodka
1 ounce Coco Lopez

pineapple and orange juice to fill
splash of grenadine
pineapple slice and cherry

Pour the first three ingredients into a tall glass of ice. Fill with the pineapple and orange juice. Splash in the grenadine. Stir. Garnish with pineapple slice and cherry.

Copabanana Split

1 ounce vanilla vodka
1 ounce strawberry vodka
1 banana, cut in half lengthwise
2 scoops vanilla ice cream
cream to blend

1 ounce dark crème de cacao
1 ounce strawberry syrup
whipped cream
nuts
maraschino cherry

Put the vodkas, half of the banana, and ice cream into a blender and blend. Slowly pour in cream until you reach a smooth consistency. Pour the dark crème de cacao in the bottom of a tall glass and insert the other banana half standing in the glass. Fill halfway with the blended mixture. Add the strawberry syrup. Continue to fill the glass with blended mixture. Add whipped cream, nuts, and a cherry on top of the drink.

Cosmopolitan

1½ ounces lemon vodka
½ ounce Cointreau
¼ ounce lime juice or freshly squeezed lime
¼ ounce cranberry juice
lemon twist, orange twist, or lime wedge

Pour all liquid ingredients into a shaker tin of ice. Shake and strain into a cocktail glass. Garnish with lemon twist, orange twist, or lime wedge.

Creamsicle

1 ounce vanilla vodka
½ ounce triple sec
orange juice and half-and-half to fill

Pour the alcohol into a tall glass. Fill with orange juice and half-and-half. Pour into a shaker. Shake, then strain into another tall glass of ice.

Death by Chocolatini

½ ounce chocolate
strawberry
chocolate syrup
1½ ounces vanilla vodka
1½ ounces chocolate liqueur
2 ounces cream

Melt the chocolate in a microwave; then dip the strawberry in the chocolate. Cool in the freezer. Swirl chocolate syrup inside a martini glass. Set the martini glass in the freezer. Pour the vodka, liqueur, and cream into a shaker tin. Shake, then strain into the chilled glass. Garnish the rim with the chocolate-covered strawberry.

🍸 Dirty Girl Scout Cookie

1 ounce vodka
1 ounce coffee liqueur

1 ounce Irish cream liqueur
¼ ounce green crème de menthe

Combine ingredients in a shaker half filled with ice. Shake well. Strain into an old-fashioned glass with ice.

Salty Snacks

Back in saloon times, proprietors offered free lunches, most of which were overly salted, forcing the thirsty diner to buy an alcoholic drink. Many bars now offer peanuts and salty snacks for the same reason.

Florida Sunset

1½ ounces orange-flavored vodka
½ ounce grenadine

orange juice to fill
orange slice

Fill a tall glass with ice. Pour in the orange-flavored vodka and the grenadine. Slowly fill the glass with orange juice. The result will be a red layer on the bottom mixing with the orange layer. Garnish with an orange slice.

Georgia Peach

1½ ounces peach vodka
1 ounce peach-flavored brandy
¼ ounce lemon juice

1 teaspoon peach preserves
½ fresh peach, cut up

Combine ingredients in a blender with ice. Blend thoroughly. Pour into a tall glass.

Georgia Rose

sprig of mint
1½ ounces rose vodka

½ ounce peach brandy
2 ounces peach nectar

In a short glass, drop in the mint and pour in the rose vodka. Muddle. Pour the minted rose vodka, peach brandy, and peach nectar in a shaker of ice. Shake and strain over a short glass of crushed ice.

Greyhound

1½ ounces vodka

grapefruit juice to fill

Fill a glass of your choice with ice and pour in the vodka, then fill with grapefruit juice.

Hairy Navel

1 ounce vodka
1 ounce peach schnapps

fresh orange juice to fill

Pour the vodka and peach schnapps into a highball glass of ice. Fill with orange juice.

Wet Your Whistle

One common explanation for the origin of this phrase is that English pubs used to have cups with whistles built into them. A patron in need of a refill would use the whistle to get the barmaid's attention. However, you'd be hard-pressed to find any of these whistling vessels in London today—probably because they never existed in the first place. There is no archaeological evidence of these cups.

Harvey Wallbanger

1½ ounces vodka
orange juice to fill

1 ounce Galliano

Pour vodka into a tall glass of ice. Fill with orange juice to a half-inch from the rim. Top with the Galliano.

Hollywood

1 ounce vodka
1 ounce raspberry liqueur

pineapple juice to fill

Pour the vodka and raspberry liqueur into a highball glass of ice. Fill with pineapple juice.

Hunka Hunka Burning Love

1 ounce raspberry rum or vodka
1 ounce hazelnut liqueur
½ ounce raspberry liqueur
2 scoops banana ice cream

milk to blend
half a banana
1 ounce 151 rum

Put the raspberry rum or vodka, hazelnut liqueur, raspberry liqueur, and banana ice cream into a blender. Add the milk little by little to reach a smooth consistency. Pour into a tall glass and stick the banana into the glass standing up. Pour the 151 rum all over the banana and light.

I Dream of Genie Martini

2 ounces cherry-flavored vodka
3 ounces pink lemonade
splash of grenadine for color
large cube of food-grade dry ice

Shake the first three ingredients in a shaker tin of ice. Strain into a martini glass. Using tongs, drop in a large cube of food-grade dry ice to activate your Genie Martini. Do not touch or drink the ice. Use a cocktail straw in your martini glass as a safety precaution.

Itsy Bitsy Teenie Weenie Yellow Polka Dot Martini

½ ounce dark chocolate
1 ounce raspberry or strawberry vodka
1 ounce limoncello
1 ounce lemon juice
½ ounce simple syrup

Melt the dark chocolate in the microwave. Carefully dip your finger in the chocolate and make polka dots on the inside of a martini glass. Set the glass in the freezer for a minute to harden the chocolate. In a shaker tin of ice add the other ingredients. Shake, then strain into the glass.

Dry Ice

Dry ice is frozen carbon dioxide (the stuff you breathe out). You buy it from your local ice company. The most common use is to put a chunk of it in a punch to get an eerie foggy effect. Keep dry ice chunks as large as possible because you never want to swallow it. Also, you never want to store it in an airtight container or touch it with your bare hands, especially if they're wet. Follow these simple precautions and you'll be fine.

🍸 Lemondrop Martini

sugar
1½ ounces citrus-flavored vodka
½ ounce triple sec or Cointreau
1 ounce lemon juice
½ ounce simple syrup
sugar-coated lemon wedge

Rim a martini glass with sugar. Pour liquid ingredients into a shaker. Shake, then strain into the glass. Garnish with a sugar-coated lemon wedge set on the rim.

Lemon Love Shack Shake

1 ounce lemon vodka   2 ounces cream
1 ounce Cointreau   1 big scoop Italian lemon ice

Put all ingredients into a blender and blend. Add more lemon ice for more of a lemony taste. To make it creamier, add more cream.

Liquid Viagra

1 ounce vodka   ½ ounce apricot brandy
½ ounce blue curaçao   ½ ounce lime juice

This drink can be made on the rocks or straight up. Pour all ingredients into a shaker tin of ice. Shake, then strain into a glass of your choice with or without ice.

Love Potion #9

1 ounce mandarin vodka   white (clear) cranberry juice to fill
1 ounce Parfait Amor   sprig of purple seedless grapes

Pour vodka and Parfait Amour into a tall glass of ice. Fill with white cranberry juice. Garnish with the grapes.

Madras

1½ ounces vodka
orange and cranberry juice to fill

Pour the vodka into a highball glass of ice. Fill with the juices. Stir.

Mango Heat Wave

2 ounces mandarin vodka
1 ounce Passoã passion fruit liqueur
2 ounces mango nectar
2 ounces sweet-and-sour mix
paper parasol

Put a cup of ice into a blender; then add all liquid ingredients. Blend. Pour into a tropical glass and garnish with fruits of your choice and a paper parasol.

Riddle

There are four bottles of wine in a picnic basket and four girls. Each girl takes a bottle, yet one bottle remains in the basket. How is this possible? Answer: One girl took the last bottle of wine while it was in the basket.

Melon Ball

1 ounce vodka   freshly squeezed orange juice to fill
1 ounce melon liqueur

Pour ingredients into a mixing glass nearly filled with ice. Stir, then strain into a highball glass of ice.

Melonliscious Mistress

1 ounce melon liqueur
1 ounce lemon vodka or rum

7-Up to fill
maraschino cherry

Pour melon liqueur and vodka or rum into a tall glass of ice.
Fill with 7-Up and stir. Garnish with a maraschino cherry.

Metropolitan

1½ ounces vodka
½ ounce crème de framboise (raspberry liqueur)
1 ounce cranberry juice
¼ ounce fresh lime juice
raspberry

Pour liquid ingredients into a shaker full of ice. Shake, then
strain into a chilled cocktail glass. Garnish with a raspberry.

Moscow Mule

2 ounces Smirnoff vodka
1 ounce fresh lime juice

ginger beer to fill

Pour ingredients into a highball glass nearly filled with ice.
Stir well.

Mudslide

1 ounce vodka
½ ounce coffee liqueur
½ ounce Irish cream

half-and-half to fill
chocolate syrup and whipped
    cream (if frozen)

This drink can be made on the rocks or frozen. If making on the
rocks, pour vodka, coffee liqueur, Irish cream, and half-and-half
into a short glass of ice. Pour into a shaker. Shake and pour
back into the glass. If making frozen, pour the same ingredients
into a blender with a cup of ice. Blend, then pour into a tall
chocolate-swirled glass and top off with whipped cream.

Passion Cup

2 ounces vodka
2 ounces orange juice
1 ounce passion fruit juice

½ ounce coconut cream
maraschino cherry

Combine liquid ingredients in a shaker half filled with ice. Shake well. Strain into a large wine glass. Top with a cherry.

Peaches and Creamtini

1½ ounces orange vodka
1½ ounces peach schnapps

2 ounces orange juice
splash of cream

Pour all ingredients into a shaker tin of ice. Shake, then strain into a martini glass.

Maraschino Cherries
Don't infuse alcohol with maraschino cherries with the goal of getting maraschino cherry–flavored vodka or rum. These cherries aren't real. They are made by taking real cherries, pitting them, and bleaching them white. The cherries are then dyed with red color #40.

Pearl Harbor

1½ ounces vodka
½ ounce melon liqueur

pineapple juice to fill

Pour the vodka and melon liqueur into a highball glass of ice. Fill with pineapple juice.

Pink Cadillactini

1 ounce vanilla vodka
½ ounce Galliano
½ ounce white crème de cacao

⅛ ounce grenadine
3 ounces cream or milk

Pour all ingredients into a shaker tin of ice and shake until cold and frothy. Strain into a martini glass.

Pomegranate Martini

2 ounces citrus vodka
1 ounce pomegranate juice

½ ounce simple syrup

Shake all ingredients well with ice and strain into a chilled martini glass.

Russian Spring Punch

2 ounces vodka
¾ ounce crème de cassis
¾ ounce fresh lemon juice

½ ounce simple syrup
sparkling wine to fill
lemon wedge and two raspberries

Build over ice in a tall glass. Top with sparkling wine. Stir gently. Garnish with a lemon wedge and two raspberries.

 ## Salty Dog

salt to rim
1½ ounces vodka

grapefruit juice to fill
lime wedge

Rim a highball glass with salt. Fill with ice. Pour in the vodka and fill with grapefruit juice. Garnish with lime wedge.

> **Match Trick**
> Challenge someone to drop a paper match on the bar
> top or table top so that it lands on its side. They will try
> many times. To get it to work, take a match and bend it a
> little before dropping it. It will land on its side.

Screwdriver

1½ ounces vodka
2½ ounces freshly squeezed orange juice

Fill a glass with ice. Add the ingredients and stir.

Seabreeze

1½ ounces vodka   lime wedge
cranberry and grapefruit juice to fill

Pour into a highball glass over ice. Garnish with lime wedge.

Sex in Front of the Fireplace

1 ounce raspberry liqueur   3 miniature Tootsie Rolls
1 ounce orange vodka   ½ ounce Grand Marnier
1 ounce peach schnapps   long fireplace match
white cranberry juice
orange juice

Pour the raspberry liqueur in a tall glass; then fill with ice.
Mix the vodka and peach schnapps and slowly pour into the
glass. Gently fill with equal parts of white (clear) cranberry
and orange juice. Garnish the top of the drink with the Tootsie
Rolls, pour the Grand Marnier on top, and light.

Wine from an Empty Bottle Trick

After you finish the last drop from a bottle of wine, announce to your friends that you can drink another shot of wine from the bottle. Your friends will think it's impossible, but you can prove them wrong. Simply turn the bottle upside down, pour some wine from your glass into the punt (the indention on the bottom of the bottle), then drink. You have just drunk a shot of wine from the empty bottle.

Sex on the Beach

1½ ounces vodka
1 ounce peach schnapps

2 ounces orange juice
2 ounces cranberry juice

Combine all ingredients in a highball glass almost filled with ice. Stir.

Sloe Screw

1 ounce vodka
1 ounce sloe gin

2 ounces fresh orange juice

Pour all ingredients into a tall glass of ice and stir.

Smiling Tiger

1 ounce black vodka
½ ounce black sambuca
¼ ounce vanilla extract

1¾ ounces orange juice
cream to top

Pour black vodka, black sambuca, and vanilla extract into a tall glass (black). Fill to the top with ice and slowly fill a little more than three-quarters with orange juice (orange). To make the white stripe, slowly fill the rest of the way with cream.

Sour Apple-tini

1 ounce citrus-flavored vodka
1 ounce sour apple liqueur
2 ounces sour mix

Pour all ingredients into a shaker. Shake and strain into a martini glass.

Sloe Gin
The Sloe Screw is part of the Screwdriver family. Sloe gin is used, but it has no gin in it whatsoever. It's a red sweet liqueur flavored with blackthorn sloe plums and is aged in wood barrels.

Stupid Cupid

2 ounces pear vodka
1 ounce sloe gin
1 ounce fresh lemon juice

Pour ingredients into a mixing glass nearly filled with ice. Stir, then strain into a cocktail glass.

Upside-Down Pineapple Martini

¼ ounce grenadine
1 ounce vanilla vodka
1 ounce Irish cream
1 ounce butterscotch schnapps
2 ounces pineapple juice
maraschino cherry

Pour the grenadine into a martini glass. Pour the rest of the liquid ingredients into a shaker tin of ice. Shake, then strain into the martini glass. Drop in the cherry.

�🍸 Vodka and Tonic

2 ounces vodka
tonic water to fill
lime wedge

Fill a highball glass with ice. Pour in the vodka. Fill with tonic and garnish with the lime wedge.

🍸 Vodka Collins

2 ounces vodka
1 ounce fresh lemon juice
¼ ounce simple syrup

club soda to fill
orange slice and cherry

Shake the first three ingredients with ice. Strain into a Collins glass. Fill with club soda and garnish with an orange slice and cherry.

🍸 Vodka Gimlet

2 ounces vodka
½ ounce Rose's lime juice (or ¼ ounce fresh lime juice and
   ¼ ounce simple syrup)
lime wedge

Add all ingredients to a mixing glass half filled with ice. Shake and strain into a rocks glass of ice. Garnish with lime wedge.

Spiked Mnemonics

A mnemonic is a sentence, formula, or rhyme that helps you remember something. Here's a musical one: Easter Bunnies Get Drunk At Easter (Guitar tuning: E, B, G, D, A, E).

Vodka Martini

½ ounce dry vermouth
2 ounces vodka
two olives or lemon twist

In a mixing glass half filled with ice, add the vermouth first, then the vodka. Stir, then strain into a martini glass. Serve with two olives or a twist of lemon.

Vodka on the Rocks

2 ounces vodka
lemon twist

Place a few ice cubes in a rocks glass and add vodka. Garnish with a lemon twist.

Vodka Red Bull

2 ounces vodka
Red Bull energy drink to fill

Pour the vodka into a highball glass of ice. Fill with Red Bull.

Vodka Sour

2 ounces vodka
1 ounce fresh lemon juice
¼ ounce simple syrup
orange slice and cherry

Fill shaker glass two-thirds with ice. Add liquid ingredients and shake. Strain into a highball glass or over a short glass of ice. Garnish with an orange slice and a cherry.

White Chocolatini

1½ ounces vanilla vodka
1 ounce Godiva White Chocolate Liqueur
2 ounces cream
white chocolate shavings

Pour the liquid ingredients into a shaker tin of ice. Shake, then strain into a martini glass. Sprinkle the white chocolate shavings on top.

White Russian

1 ounce vodka
1 ounce coffee liqueur
2 ounces cream

Shake all ingredients and pour into a short glass of ice.

Woo Woo

1 ounce vodka
1 ounce peach schnapps
cranberry juice to fill

Pour the vodka and peach schnapps into a highball glass. Fill with cranberry juice.

Chapter 7

Gin: Gin Is In

In its basic form, gin is vodka that has been redistilled with herbs and botanicals. Gin-makers use citrus peels, coriander, ginger, rose petals, nutmeg, and cassia bark, but the most prominent is the juniper berry. Dr. Sylvius, a Dutch professor and physician, is credited with making gin as a cure-all tonic in the 1650s. Today, many alcohol historians debate this claim, because the juniper berry was quite plentiful in Italy, which leads them to believe that Italian monks were the first to make gin.

Gin Classifications

The three main categories of gin are London dry gin, Plymouth English gin, and genever (also spelled jenever). The word *genever* is Dutch for juniper, and the word *gin* is a shortening of the Dutch term. Holland and Belgium make genever, which is considered the original style of gin made in pot stills. It's sweeter than London dry gin. London dry gin is the most popular because it mixes well. It doesn't have to be made in England (the United States, Germany, and Spain make gin as well). Plymouth English gin can only be made in Plymouth, England—and it was the first gin used in a printed recipe in a Martini.

Kitty Cat Gin

Old Tom Gin is the only produced example we have today of what sweeter gin used to taste like. It got its name from a cat-shaped plaque that was mounted on the outside of some English pubs. One could deposit money in the cat's mouth and then place their mouth on a tube between the cats paws. A barman inside would pour a dram of gin into the tube. How about that for an ancient vending machine!

Alaska

| 1½ ounces gin | 2 dashes orange bitters |
| ½ ounce yellow Chartreuse | cherry |

Shake the liquid ingredients in a shaker tin of ice. Strain into a martini glass. Garnish with cherry.

Alexander

1 ounce gin
1 ounce crème de cacao

1 ounce sweet cream

Shake ingredients in a shaker of ice. Strain into a martini glass.

Apple Ginger Gin

2 ounces London dry gin
2 ounces apple juice

ginger beer to fill

Pour the gin and apple juice into a tall glass. Fill with ginger beer. Stir.

Aviation

2 ounces gin
1 ounce maraschino liqueur

1 ounce fresh lemon juice
lemon twist

Shake all liquid ingredients in a shaker tin of ice. Strain into a martini glass. Garnish with a lemon twist.

Maraschino Liqueur
Maraschino liqueur is made from crushed Dalmatian marasca cherries. The pits, stems, and seeds are also used. It's clear and has a neutral grain spirit base.

Bee's Knees

2 ounces gin
¾ ounce honey

½ ounce fresh lemon juice

Shake all ingredients in a shaker tin of ice. Strain into a martini glass.

A Businessman Walks into a Bar and Orders a Martini
A businessman walks into a bar and orders a Martini. After he finishes the drink, he peeks inside his shirt pocket and orders another Martini. After he finishes that one, he again peeks inside his shirt pocket and orders yet another Martini. The bartender finally asks the man why he keeps looking inside his shirt before ordering. The man says, "I'm peeking at a photo of my wife. When she starts to look good, then I know it's time to go home."

Belgian Brownie

1 ounce genever
1 ounce white crème de cacao
½ ounce cognac
cream to fill

Pour the first three ingredients into a highball glass. Fill with cream. Stir.

Bermuda Rose

1¼ ounces dry gin
¼ ounce apricot nectar liqueur
¼ ounce grenadine

Shake ingredients in a shaker of ice. Strain into a martini glass.

Bijou

1 ounce Plymouth gin
1 ounce green chartreuse
1 ounce sweet vermouth
dash orange bitters

Shake all ingredients in a shaker tin of ice. Strain into a martini glass.

Booming Gin

2 ounces London dry gin
1 ounce elderflower liqueur
Perrier to fill

Pour gin and elderflower liqueur into a highball glass. Fill with Perrier. Stir.

Bramble

1½ ounces gin
1 ounce fresh lime juice
½ ounce simple syrup

½ ounce crème de mûre
2 blackberries

Shake the gin, fresh lime juice, and simple syrup in a shaker half filled with ice. Strain into a rocks glass filled with crushed ice. Float the crème de mûre on top. Garnish with 2 blackberries.

Bronx

1 ounce dry gin
1 ounce French dry vermouth
1 ounce fresh orange juice

Shake all ingredients in a shaker tin of ice. Strain into a martini glass.

Bull Dog

1½ ounces gin
ginger ale to fill
2 ounces fresh orange juice

Pour the gin and orange juice into a highball glass. Fill with ginger ale. Stir.

Cabaret Cocktail

½ ounce gin
1 ounce absinthe substitute

2 ounces cold espresso
lemon twist

Shake all liquid ingredients in a shaker tin of ice. Strain into a martini glass. Garnish with a lemon twist.

Clover Club

2 ounces Plymouth gin
1 ounce fresh lemon juice

½ ounce grenadine
1 egg white

Shake all ingredients in a shaker tin of ice. Strain into a martini glass.

Colonial Cocktail

2 ounces gin
1 ounce grapefruit juice

½ ounce maraschino liqueur

Shake ingredients in a shaker of ice. Strain into a martini glass.

Cotton Gin

2 ounces London dry gin

1 ounce sambuca

Shake ingredients in a shaker tin of ice. Strain into a martini glass. The water from the ice will turn this drink white.

Cowboy Martini

3 ounces Plymouth gin
¼ ounce simple syrup
2 dashes orange bitters

4 or 5 mint leaves (partially torn)
orange twist

Shake all liquid ingredients and the mint in a shaker tin of ice. Strain into a martini glass. Garnish with orange twist.

Derby Cocktail

half a fresh peach, chopped
several mint leaves (save one sprig for a garnish)
½ ounce peach liqueur
2½ ounces Beefeater Gin

Muddle together peach slices, mint, and peach liqueur in a mixing glass or shaker tin. Add gin and ice, shake, then strain into a small martini glass. Garnish with a sprig of mint.

Dirty Martini

2 ounces London dry gin
½ ounce olive juice
olives

Shake liquid ingredients in a shaker tin of ice. Strain into a martini glass. Garnish with olives.

Distressed Damson

1 fresh lime, peeled and chopped
loose handful of blueberries
1½ ounces damson gin

Muddle the chopped fresh lime and blueberries in a rocks glass. Add the damson gin, stir, and top up with crushed ice.

Damson Gin
Damson gin is made from damson juice (a type of plum), gin, and cane sugar. The fruit is grown in the orchards of the Lyth Valley, Cumbria, in the United Kingdom. Walking through a damson orchard is breathtaking because of the rich purple color of the fruit.

Dry Tea

2 ounces dry gin
2 ounces cold tea

Sprite or 7-Up to fill
lemon wedge

Pour the gin and tea into a highball glass. Fill with Sprite or 7-Up. Garnish with a lemon wedge.

Dutch Breakfast

1 ounce gin
¼ ounce Galliano
1 ounce advocaat

½ ounce fresh lime juice
½ ounce fresh lemon juice
½ ounce simple syrup

Pour all ingredients into a highball glass of ice. Stir.

Dutch Trade Winds

2 ounces genever
½ ounce curaçao
½ ounce lemon juice
1 teaspoon simple syrup

Pour all ingredients into a cocktail shaker half filled with ice. Shake. Strain into a martini glass.

Floradora

1½ ounces gin
½ ounce fresh lime juice
½ ounce framboise liqueur
   or raspberry syrup

ginger ale to fill
lime wedge

Pour the first three ingredients into a highball glass. Fill with ginger ale. Garnish with lime wedge.

French 75

1 ounce gin
1 ounce lemon juice
½ ounce simple syrup

champagne to fill
lemon twist

Build into a champagne flute and top with chilled champagne.
Garnish with a lemon twist.

French 75

The French 75 is believed to have been invented by
legendary bartender Harry MacElhone in honor of the
famous French 75 light field gun. The artillery piece
was a major weapon in World War I, and the cocktail
debuted in Paris after the Great War.

French Martini

2 ounces dry gin
¼ ounce raspberry liqueur

1 ounce pineapple juice

Shake all ingredients in a shaker tin of ice. Strain into a martini
glass.

Gibson

1½ ounces dry gin
½ ounce French vermouth

3 pearl onions
lemon twist

Shake gin and vermouth in a shaker tin of ice. Strain into a
martini glass. Garnish with onions and a lemon twist.

🍸 Gimlet

2 ounces gin   ¾ ounce sweetened lime juice (or
lime wedge   fresh lime juice and simple syrup)

Shake the gin and lime juice in a shaker of ice. Strain into a
rocks glass of ice. Garnish with lime wedge.

🍸 Gin and It

2 ounces gin   ¾ ounce sweet vermouth

Pour ingredients into a mixing glass of ice and stir. Strain into
a martini glass.

Gin and Juice

1½ ounces gin   orange juice to fill

Pour the gin into a highball glass of ice. Fill with orange juice.
Stir.

Gin and Sin

2 ounces gin   ¼ ounce orange juice
¼ ounce fresh lemon juice   ¼ ounce grenadine

Shake all ingredients in a shaker of ice. Strain into a martini
glass.

🍸 Gin and Tonic

1½ ounces gin   lime wedge
tonic to fill

Pour the gin into a highball glass of ice. Fill with tonic. Garnish
with a lime wedge.

Gin Daisy

2 ounces gin
¼ ounce Grand Marnier
¼ ounce simple syrup

club soda to fill
juice of half a lemon

Combine all ingredients in a shaker of ice and shake well. Strain into large wine glass. Fill with club soda.

Gin Fizz

2 ounces genever
½ ounce fresh lemon juice
½ ounce simple syrup

half an egg white
soda water to fill
lemon wedge

Combine genever, lemon juice, syrup, and egg white in a shaker of ice. Shake well and strain into a tall glass of ice. Fill with soda water and garnish with a lemon wedge.

Gin Rickey

2 ounces gin
juice of 1 lime
club soda to fill

Shake the gin and lime juice in a shaker of ice. Strain into a highball glass of ice. Fill with club soda.

Gin Sour

2 ounces gin
1 ounce fresh lemon juice
½ ounce simple syrup
half an egg white

Shake the ingredients in a shaker of ice. Strain into a highball glass of ice.

Huckleberry Finn Gin

3 ounces huckleberry-infused genever
huckleberry bloom

Shake the huckleberry genever in a shaker tin of ice and strain into a martini glass. Garnish with a huckleberry bloom.

Homemade Infused Huckleberry Gin

Buy a bottle of genever and two pints of huckleberries (the season is mid to late summer in the United States). Next, obtain a large-mouthed glass container to make your infusion. Place the washed huckleberries in the jar; then add the genever. Close the lid tightly, remove from direct sunlight, and let sit from four days to two weeks. Strain and bottle when finished.

Jasmine

1½ ounces gin
¼ ounce Cointreau
¾ ounce freshly squeezed lemon juice
¼ ounce Campari

Shake all ingredients in a shaker of ice. Strain into a martini glass.

Jupiter Cocktail

1½ ounces Plymouth gin
½ ounce dry vermouth
¼ ounce fresh orange juice
¼ ounce Parfait Amour (violet liqueur)

Shake all ingredients in a shaker of ice. Strain into a martini glass.

Looney Bin Gin

3 ounces Seagram's Orange Twist gin

Shake the gin in a shaker of ice. Strain into a martini glass.

Martinez

2 ounces Martini & Rossi red vermouth
1 ounce Tanqueray Ten gin
2 dashes Luxardo maraschino liqueur
dash angostura bitters

Stir all ingredients in a mixing glass of ice. Strain into a martini glass.

Martini

2 ounces gin
⅛ ounce dry vermouth
2 large pimiento-stuffed green olives

Shake gin and vermouth in a shaker of ice. Strain into a martini glass. Garnish with the olives. Some people pour the dry vermouth into a mister and mist the top of the martini.

King of Cocktails

By far, the Martini is the king of cocktails. It is the icon of the cocktail culture and whole books have been written about its simplicity—with a dash of controversy. You should know that no one knows when, who, or where the first Martini was created. What we do know is that Jerry Thomas published a cocktail recipe called a Martinez in *The Bartenders Guide* in 1887.

Million-Dollar Cocktail

1½ ounces gin
1 ounce sweet vermouth
1½ ounces pineapple juice
½ ounce fresh lemon juice
1 ounce cream
¼ ounce simple syrup
¼ ounce grenadine

Shake all ingredients with ice and strain into a martini glass.

Monkey Gland

2 ounces gin
1 ounce orange juice
1 dash Pernod
¼ ounce grenadine
orange twist

Shake all liquid ingredients with ice and strain into a martini glass. Garnish with an orange twist.

Negroni

1 ounce gin
1 ounce sweet vermouth
1 ounce Campari
lemon twist

Pour liquid ingredients into a shaker. Shake and strain into a rocks glass of ice. Garnish with a lemon twist.

Ninja Turtle

1 ounce gin
½ ounce blue curaçao
fresh orange juice to fill

Pour the gin and curaçao into a highball glass of ice. Fill with orange juice.

☿ Pegu Club

2 ounces dry gin
1 ounce curaçao
dash angostura bitters

dash orange bitters
¼ ounce lime juice

Pour the ingredients into a shaker with ice. Shake, then strain into a martini glass.

The Pegu Club

The original Pegu Club entertained British colonial officers stationed in Burma in the late nineteenth and early twentieth centuries. It was renowned for its cocktails, and its house drink gained worldwide popularity by the 1930s. The club has closed, but half a world away, master bartender Audrey Saunders has introduced a Pegu Club in New York City. The new Pegu Club strives to make cocktails the way they were supposed to be made, with fresh ingredients and a commitment to superior mixology.

☿ Pink Gin

2 to 3 ounces gin

3 or 4 dashes angostura bitters

Pour the ingredients into a shaker with ice. Shake, then strain into a martini glass.

☿ Pink Lady

1½ ounces gin
¼ ounce grenadine

1 egg white
¼ ounce sweet cream

Shake well with ice. Strain into a martini glass.

Pirates Sour

2 ounces dry gin
1½ ounces sour mix

3 dashes angostura bitters
float of Goldschläger

Shake the first three ingredients with ice. Strain into a sour glass or rocks glass and float the Goldschläger on top.

Ramos Gin Fizz

1½ ounces gin
½ ounce fresh lemon juice
½ ounce fresh lime juice
1¼ ounces simple syrup

2 ounces milk
1 egg white
2 drops orange flower water
club soda to fill

Shake all ingredients except the club soda with ice. Strain into a highball glass without ice. Fill with club soda.

The Ramos Gin Fizz

The Ramos Gin Fizz proudly traces its roots to New Orleans, where it was created in the 1880s by Henry C. Ramos. It uses milk and egg white to complement the traditional gin/juice/syrup base. The orange flower water gives the drink its unique exotic taste. Orange flower water isn't a common ingredient, but you can find it at specialty grocery stores and online retail sites.

Raspberry Collins

2 ounces Plymouth gin
¾ ounce raspberry liqueur
1 ounce fresh lemon juice
½ ounce simple syrup

½ ounce raspberry purée
club soda to fill
lemon slice and 2 raspberries

Shake all the liquid ingredients except the club soda with ice. Strain into a tall glass of ice. Fill with club soda. Garnish with lemon slice and raspberries.

Original Red Snapper

2 ounces gin
Bloody Mary mix to fill

Pour the gin into a tall glass and fill with the mix. Gently roll into another glass and back again. Garnish with celery, lime, or whatever you desire.

Rusty Windmill

1 ounce genever
1 ounce Drambuie

Pour the ingredients into a rocks glass of ice.

Shore Breeze

1½ ounces gin   tonic to fill
2 ounces grapefruit juice

Pour the gin and grapefruit juice into a highball glass of ice. Fill with tonic.

Singapore Sling

1½ ounces gin   club soda to fill
2 ounces sour mix   ½ ounce cherry brandy

Shake the gin and sour mix with ice. Strain into a tall glass of ice. Fill with club soda. Float the cherry brandy.

Singapore Sling #2

1½ ounces gin
½ ounce Cherry Heering
½ ounce Cointreau
½ ounce Bénédictine

½ ounce pineapple juice
½ ounce fresh lime juice
½ ounce grenadine
dash bitters

Pour all ingredients into a shaker of ice. Shake. Strain into a tall glass of ice.

Skip and Go Naked

½ ounce gin
½ ounce sweet-and-sour mix
beer to fill

Shake the gin and sweet-and-sour mix with ice. Pour into a highball glass of ice. Fill with beer.

Stork Club Cocktail

1½ ounces gin
½ ounce Cointreau
¼ ounce fresh lime juice

1 ounce fresh orange juice
dash angostura bitters
orange twist

Shake all liquid ingredients with ice. Strain into a martini glass. Garnish with an orange twist.

Straits Sling

2 ounces Plymouth gin
¼ ounce kirschwasser
¼ ounce Bénédictine
1 ounce fresh lemon juice

2 dashes angostura bitters
2 dashes orange bitters
soda water to top
orange slice

Build over ice in a tall glass. Top with soda water. Garnish with an orange slice.

> **Liquid Beauty**
> Some homemade shampoo and conditioner recipes call for common alcohols such as gin, rum, and vodka. If you look at the ingredients in your current shampoo and conditioner, you'll almost certainly find alcohol—although not the kind you'd like to drink!

Strike's On

2 ounces genever
½ ounce lemon juice
⅓ ounce pineapple syrup
1½ ounces sparkling apple juice
lemon slice

Shake all liquid ingredients except sparkling apple juice and strain into an old-fashioned glass filled with broken ice. Add sparkling apple juice and slice of lemon, and serve.

Thin Gin

2 ounces dry gin
diet ginger ale to fill

Pour the gin into a highball glass of ice. Fill with diet ginger ale.

Tom Collins

1½ ounces gin
2 ounces sweet-and-sour mix (or fresh lime juice and simple syrup)
club soda to fill
orange slice and cherry

Combine gin and sweet-and-sour mix in a shaker. Shake and strain into a Collins glass of ice. Fill with club soda. Garnish with an orange and cherry.

The Wet Spot

1½ ounces Plymouth gin
½ ounce apricot brandy
1 ounce apple juice
½ ounce elderflower syrup
lemon twist

Shake this award-winning cocktail by Will Shine Aisha Sharpe with ice. Strain into a martini glass. Garnish with a lemon twist.

NASCAR

During Prohibition, bootleggers carrying moonshine would soup up their car engines in order to outrun the police. After Prohibition, they raced each other on country roads for the fun of it. These were the humble offshoot beginnings of NASCAR. A legendary moonshiner by the name of Junior Johnson was one of NASCAR's first drivers.

White Lady

1½ ounces Plymouth Gin
¾ ounce Cointreau
¾ ounce fresh lemon juice
lemon twist

Shake with ice. Strain into a chilled martini glass. Garnish with a lemon twist.

Chapter 8

Rum:
How Sweet It Is

Rum is a spirit distilled from sugar cane and its by-products—sugar cane juice or molasses. It's produced in hot climates. It comes in three styles: white (light), gold (aged), and dark.

Rum History

Beginning in the 1600s, members of the British Royal Navy received a half pint of rum a day to ward off scurvy. It didn't work (scurvy is caused by a vitamin C deficiency), but Britannia did rule the oceans for many years. The rum the British soldiers drank was a crude alcohol that bears little resemblance to the spirit we enjoy today. We owe the transformation to a family by the name of Bacardi. In the 1800s, a Spanish wine merchant named Don Facundo Bacardí moved with his family to Cuba. He and his brother José opened a small store and developed a passion for making rum. They were determined to create the first smooth rum. The result was Bacardi rum, and today it's the most popular rum in the world.

The Real McCoy

In rum-running times, captains would add water to the rum bottles to stretch their profits. Captain McCoy was one captain who did not cut his rum, and one theory states that's where we get the phrase "The Real McCoy."

Admiral Nelson's Brew

1 ounce spiced rum
½ ounce applejack
hot apple cider to fill

Pour the rum and applejack into a coffee mug and fill with hot apple cider.

Almond Joytini

1 ounce coconut rum   1 ounce crème de cacao
1 ounce amaretto   2 ounces cream

Pour all ingredients into a shaker tin of ice. Shake, then strain into a martini glass.

Bacardi Cocktail

1½ ounces Bacardi light rum   1 ounce simple syrup
¾ ounce fresh lemon juice   2 dashes grenadine

Shake all ingredients with ice. Strain into a cocktail glass.

Bahama Mama

1 ounce light rum
1 ounce dark rum
2 ounces piña colada mix
2 ounces bar punch mix (a mix of orange juice, pineapple juice, sour mix, and grenadine)
pineapple slice and cherry

Pour the rums and mixes into blender with a cup of ice. Blend, then pour into a tropical glass. Garnish with pineapple slice and cherry.

Banana Boat

1 ounce light rum
1 ounce crème de banana
1 ounce white crème de cacao
2 scoops vanilla ice cream

Blend ingredients in a blender. Pour into a tropical glass.

Banana Daiquiri

1 ounce light rum
¾ ounce fresh lime juice
2 ounces simple syrup
½ ounce banana liqueur
½ small banana (save a slice for a garnish)

Blend ingredients in a blender. Pour into a tropical glass. Garnish with slice of banana.

Banana Popsicle

1 ounce Cabana Boy banana rum
1 ounce crème de banana
1 ounce simple syrup
1 ounce water
paper parasol

Blend liquid ingredients in a blender. Pour into a tropical glass. Garnish with paper parasol.

Bermuda Triangle Tea

1 ounce Bermuda Black Seal rum
1 ounce Puerto Rican Bacardi light rum
equal amounts of Florida orange juice and sweet-and-sour
    mix to fill
paper parasol

Fill a tall glass with ice and pour in all the liquid ingredients. Garnish with paper parasol.

Between the Sheets

¾ ounce light rum
¾ ounce brandy
¾ ounce triple sec

½ ounce lemon juice
lemon twist

Shake with ice. Strain into a martini glass. Garnish with a lemon twist.

Mind Your P's and Q's
We get the phrase "mind your P's and Q's" from old English pubs. In old England, patrons ordered ale in pints and quarts. When they got unruly, the bartender would yell at them to mind their own pints and quarts and settle down.

Blackberry Mojito

5 blackberries
3 sprigs of mint (one for a garnish)
½ fresh lime, chopped

1 ounce simple syrup
1½ ounces light rum
club soda to fill

Muddle the blackberries, mint, lime, and simple syrup in a mixing glass. Add the rum. Shake in a shaker tin of ice. Strain into a highball glass of cracked ice. Fill with club soda. Garnish with a mint sprig.

Blue Hawaiian

1 ounce light rum
1 ounce blue curaçao

pineapple juice to fill
pineapple slice

Pour the liquid ingredients into a highball glass of ice. Stir and garnish with pineapple slice.

☝ Bolo

2 ounces light rum
1 ounce lime juice or juice of half a lime
1 ounce orange juice
1 teaspoon fine sugar

Combine ingredients in a shaker nearly filled with ice. Strain into a cocktail glass.

Bon Bon

capful vanilla extract
¼ ounce fresh lemon juice
¼ ounce simple syrup
3 strawberries

1½ ounces cherry rum
½ ounce dark chocolate liqueur
club soda to fill

Muddle the vanilla extract, lemon juice, simple syrup, and strawberries in a mixing glass. Add the rum, chocolate liqueur, and some ice. Shake and strain into a highball glass of ice. Fill with club soda.

Brazilian Breakfast

1½ ounces cachaça
½ ounce peach brandy
1 teaspoon brown sugar

1 ounce fresh grapefruit juice
1 ounce apple juice

Shake all ingredients with ice. Strain into a short glass of ice.

Cachaça
Cachaça (cuh-SHA-suh) is Brazilian rum made from sugar cane juice. Portuguese settlers of Brazil began making it in the 1500s. There are around 4,000 brands of cachaça in Brazil.

Bushwacker

2 ounces dark rum   4 ounces piña colada mix
1 ounce coffee liqueur

Blend in a blender with a cup of ice. Pour into a tall glass.

Caipirinha

½ lime, chopped   2 ounces cachaça
1 teaspoon granulated sugar

Muddle the lime and sugar in a mixing glass. Add the cachaça
and ice. Shake, then strain into a rocks glass of cracked ice.

Captain's Blood

1½ ounces dark rum   2 dashes angostura bitters
¼ ounce lime juice   lemon peel spiral
¼ ounce simple syrup

Shake all liquid ingredients with ice. Strain into a short glass of
ice. Garnish with a spiral of lemon peel.

Caribbean Eclipse

2 ounces Mount Gay Eclipse rum   1 ounce fresh lime juice
1 ounce dark crème de cacao   ½ ounce simple syrup

Shake all ingredients with ice. Strain into a martini glass.

Chocolate Coco

2 ounces Bacardi Coco
1 ounce white crème de cacao
1 ounce cream

Shake all ingredients with ice. Strain into a martini glass.

Cuba Libre (Rum and Coke)

2 lime wedges
2 ounces Cuban rum
cola to fill

Fill a highball glass with ice. Squeeze the juice of one of the lime wedges over the ice and discard the wedge. Pour in the rum and fill with cola. Squeeze the second lime wedge into the drink. Swipe the rim with the lime and drop it into the drink.

Daiquiri

1½ ounces light rum
1 ounce simple syrup
¾ ounce fresh lime juice

Shake all ingredients with ice. Strain into a martini glass.

Dark 'n Stormy

2 ounces Gosling's dark rum
ginger beer to fill
lime wedge

Pour the rum over ice in a highball glass and fill with ginger beer. Squeeze in a lime wedge.

Eggnog Grog

1½ ounces dark rum
eggnog to fill
nutmeg

Pour the dark rum into a short or tall glass of your choice and fill with eggnog. This depends if you want the drink to taste strong or weak. If the eggnog is cold, you won't need to add ice. Garnish with a pinch of nutmeg on top.

First Kiss

1½ ounces coconut rum
1½ ounces pineapple juice

1 ounce milk
¼ ounce grenadine

Shake ingredients with ice. Strain into a chilled martini glass.

Flamingo

1½ ounces light rum
1½ ounces pineapple juice

¼ ounce fresh lime juice
¼ ounce grenadine

Shake ingredients well with ice. Serve in a martini glass.

Forbidden Fruit

1 ounce spiced rum
1 ounce apple schnapps

¼ ounce cinnamon schnapps
7-Up to fill

Pour the first three ingredients into a glass of ice. Fill with 7-Up.

Gingered Apple

1½ ounces apple rum
1 ounce pear purée

1 ounce fresh lemon juice
ginger beer to fill

Pour the first three ingredients into a tall glass of ice. Fill with ginger beer.

Goin' Coconutini

1 teaspoon corn syrup
shredded coconut

2 ounces coconut rum
3 ounces white (clear) cranberry juice

Pour the corn syrup onto one saucer and shredded coconut onto another. Turn your martini glass upside down and dip the rim into each. Shake rum and juice; strain into the glass.

Hawaiian Volcano

1 ounce dark rum
½ ounce 151 rum

2 ounces Passoã passion fruit liqueur
4 ounces Piña Colada mix

Blend all ingredients with ice. Pour into a tropical glass.

Hemingway Daiquiri

1 ounce light rum
¼ ounce maraschino liqueur
½ ounce grapefruit juice

¾ ounce simple syrup
¾ ounce fresh lime juice

Shake all ingredients well with ice. Serve in a martini glass.

Hot Buttered Rum

1 ounce dark rum or spiced rum
1 tablespoon hot buttered rum mix (see recipe, page 265)
hot water to fill

Pour all ingredients in an Irish coffee mug. Stir.

Hot Buttered Sugarplum Rum

1 ounce dark rum
½ ounce plum liqueur
2 tablespoons of hot buttered rum mix (see recipe, page 265)
hot water to fill

Pour all ingredients in an Irish coffee mug. Stir.

Hot Gingerbread Toddy

½ cup water
1-inch knob ginger, thinly sliced
⅛ cup sugar

1 ounce light rum
1 cup hot apple cider

Combine the water and ginger in a saucepan and bring to a boil. Remove from heat. Cover and steep 30 minutes. Add the sugar and boil again, stirring until the sugar dissolves. Strain ¼ cup into a mug, then add the rum. Fill with hot apple cider.

ᵧ Hurricane

1 ounce light rum
1 ounce dark rum
1 ounce passion fruit juice

bar punch to fill
orange slice and cherry

Combine the liquid ingredients in a shaker. Shake and strain into a tall glass or a hurricane glass of ice. Garnish with orange slice and cherry.

Pat O'Brien's

The most famous bar in New Orleans, Pat O'Brien's, invented the Hurricane. During WWII, whiskey was in low supply but there was plenty of rum. Pat made up this drink so he could sell all the rum. The hurricane glass is modeled after a hurricane lamp.

In the Mood

1 tablespoon hot chocolate mix
1 ounce dark rum

1 ounce dark crème de cacao
3 ounces cream or milk

Dip the rim of a martini glass in water, then dip it into the powdered hot chocolate mix. Pour the rum, crème de cacao, and
cream or milk into a shaker tin of ice. Shake and strain into the
rimmed martini glass.

Italian Breeze

1 ounce light rum
1 ounce Disaronno amaretto

½ ounce pineapple juice
½ ounce cranberry juice

Shake all ingredients. Strain into a chilled martini glass.

Jamaican Me Crazy

1 ounce light rum
1 ounce coconut rum
1 ounce banana liqueur

½ ounce cranberry juice
½ ounce pineapple juice
cherry

Combine and shake the liquid ingredients. Strain into a tall
glass of ice. Garnish with the cherry.

Jolly Roger

2 ounces light rum
2 ounces Drambuie

1 ounce fresh lime juice
club soda to fill

Combine the first three ingredients and shake well with ice.
Strain into a highball glass of ice. Fill with club soda.

Knickerbocker

2 ounces Appleton rum
½ ounce orange curaçao
½ ounce raspberry syrup

¾ ounce fresh lemon juice
lemon wedge

Stir all ingredients with ice in a mixing glass. Strain into a chilled martini glass.

Latitude Attitude Adjuster

½ ounce 151 rum half glass any beer
½ ounce amaretto half glass orange juice

Fill a tall glass with beer and orange juice. Set aside. Pour the 151 rum and amaretto into a shot glass. Hold the shot glass in one hand and the tall glass in the other, drop the shot into the glass, and chug the entire drink.

Lava Colada

1 ounce raspberry rum 1 ounce raspberry syrup
4 ounces piña colada mix

Blend the rum and piña colada mix with a cup of ice. Pour the raspberry syrup in the bottom of a tropical glass. Pour the blended mixture on top. The syrup will ooze up the sides.

Lemon Chiffon Pie

1 ounce light rum 2 scoops vanilla ice cream
1 ounce white crème de cacao 1 ounce fresh lemon juice

Blend all ingredients with ice. Pour into a tropical glass.

Lounge Lizard

1½ ounces dark rum
½ ounce amaretto
cola to fill

Pour the rum and amaretto in a highball glass of ice. Fill with cola.

Mai Tai Me Up

1 ounce dark rum
½ ounce light rum
1 ounce pineapple juice
1 ounce fresh lemon juice
½ ounce simple syrup
1 slice canned pineapple
maraschino cherry

Shake all ingredients in a cocktail shaker with ice. Strain in a martini glass.

A Man Walked into a Bar

A man walked into a bar and ordered Martini after Martini, each time removing the olives and placing them in a jar. When the jar was filled with olives, the man started to leave. The bartender asked him what that was all about, and he said, "My wife just sent me out for a jar of olives."

Mary Pickford

2 ounces light rum
1½ ounces pineapple juice
¼ ounce grenadine
¼ ounce maraschino liqueur

Shake all ingredients with ice. Strain into a chilled martini glass.

Mojito

3 sprigs mint (one for a garnish)
½ lime, cut
2 teaspoons of sugar
1½ ounces light rum
club soda to fill

Muddle 2 sprigs of mint, lime, and sugar in a mixing glass. Add the rum. Shake in a shaker tin with ice, then strain into a highball glass of cracked ice. Fill with club soda and garnish with a mint sprig.

007 Does It Again

In the film *Die Another Day* (2002), James Bond drinks Bollinger champagne, Havana rum, two vodka Martinis (one with an olive), and a Mojito. The Mojito's popularity exploded soon after.

Navy Grogg

1½ ounces Mount Gay Eclipse rum
1½ ounces orange curaçao
¾ ounce fresh lime juice
2 ounces fresh orange juice
dash angostura bitters

Combine all ingredients and shake well with ice. Strain into a chilled martini glass.

Olympia

3 ounces dark rum
1 ounce cherry brandy
1 ounce fresh lime juice

Shake all ingredients with ice. Strain into a chilled martini glass.

Painkiller

2 ounces Pusser's rum
4 ounces piña colada mix

1 ounce fresh orange juice
sprinkle of nutmeg

Blend all liquid ingredients with ice. Pour into a tropical glass.
Sprinkle with nutmeg.

Paradise under a Coconut Tree

coconut
hacksaw or band saw
2 ounces coconut rum
1 ounce light rum
3 ounces Coco Lopez

3 ounces pineapple juice
2 ounces cream
¼ ounce vanilla extract
paper parasol

Make a coconut cup by cutting the top off a coconut with a
band saw. The milk will spill out so have a towel handy. There
is no need to chip out the white coconut meat. Pour the coconut rum, light rum, Coco Lopez, pineapple juice, cream, and
vanilla extract into a blender. Blend with a cup of ice. Pour
into the coconut cup and garnish with a paper parasol.

Peaches at the Beaches

2 ounces peach schnapps
1 ounce light rum
¼ ounce grenadine

orange juice to fill
paper parasol

Pour the peach schnapps, light rum, and grenadine into a tall
glass of ice. Fill with orange juice. Garnish with a paper parasol

Piña Colada

1½ ounces light rum
3 ounces pineapple juice

1 ounce Coco Lopez
pineapple slice

Put the liquid ingredients into a blender with some ice. Blend
and pour into a tropical glass. Garnish with pineapple.

Pineapple Mist

2 ounces light rum
3 ounces pineapple juice

maraschino cherry

Combine rum and juice in a blender with ice. Blend thoroughly. Pour into a cocktail glass and serve with a cherry.

Pineapple Mojito

3 sprigs mint (one for garnish)
half a lime, chopped
2 pieces fresh pineapple

2 teaspoons of sugar
1½ ounces light rum
club soda to fill

Muddle 2 sprigs of mint, lime, pineapple, and sugar in a mixing glass. Add the rum. Shake in a shaker tin of ice, then strain into a highball glass of cracked ice. Fill with club soda and garnish with a mint sprig.

A Man Walks into a Bar

A man walks into a bar and sits down next to a lady and a dog. The man asks, "Does your dog bite?" The lady answers, "Never!" The man reaches out to pet the dog and the dog bites him. The man says, "I thought you said your dog doesn't bite!" The woman replies, "He doesn't. This isn't my dog."

Planter's Punch

2 ounces dark rum
bar punch mix to fill

orange slice and cherry

Combine liquid ingredients and shake, then strain into a tall glass of ice. Garnish with an orange slice and a cherry.

Rockapolitan

1 ounce Cruzan citrus rum
1 ounce Cruzan orange rum
¼ ounce fresh lime juice
¼ ounce cranberry juice

Shake all ingredients in a cocktail shaker with ice. Strain into a martini glass.

Rum Runner

1 ounce dark rum
½ ounce 151 rum
½ ounce crème de banana
½ ounce blackberry brandy
½ ounce grenadine
½ ounce Rose's lime juice
cherry

Put all liquid ingredients into a blender with some ice. Blend and pour into a tropical glass. Garnish with a cherry.

Scorpion

1 ounce light rum
1 ounce brandy
½ ounce amaretto
¾ ounce fresh lemon juice
½ ounce simple syrup
1 ounce fresh orange juice
pineapple slice and cherry

Combine all liquid ingredients and shake with ice. Strain into a tall glass of ice. Garnish with pineapple slice and cherry.

Sex with the Captain

1½ ounces Captain Morgan spiced rum
½ ounce peach schnapps
cranberry and orange juice to fill

Fill a tall glass with ice. Pour in the Captain Morgan and peach schnapps. Fill with equal parts cranberry and orange juice. Stir.

Sonora

1½ ounces light rum
½ ounce applejack
½ ounce apricot-flavored brandy
1 ounce fresh lemon juice

Shake ingredients with ice. Strain into a martini glass.

Spicy Pear

1½ ounces Captain Morgan's spiced rum
½ ounce Goldschläger
1 ounce pear purée
1 ounce apple juice
thinly sliced gingerroot

Combine all ingredients in a shaker with ice. Shake hard, then strain into a highball glass of crushed ice.

Captain Morgan

Captain Henry Morgan was a real person. The English monarchy hired the Welshman to attack Spanish ships in the Caribbean—and that he did. He also raped, tortured, burned, looted, robbed, and murdered anyone in his way for gold, jewels, or anything of value.

Strawberry Daiquiri

1½ ounces light rum
4 ounces strawberry mix
strawberry, lime wedge, sugared rim, or whipped cream
   with a cherry on top

Put the liquid ingredients into a blender with some ice. Blend and pour into a tropical glass. Garnish.

Think Pink

1½ ounces raspberry rum
½ ounce Passoã passion fruit liqueur
Sprite or 7-Up to fill

Pour the rum and Passoã into a highball glass of ice. Fill with Sprite or 7-Up. Stir.

Truffle

1½ ounces Gosling's Black Seal rum
½ ounce Cherry Heering
½ ounce maple syrup
1 ounce cold espresso

Shake all ingredients in a cocktail shaker with ice. Strain into a martini glass.

Strawberry Mix

Most bars have a strawberry mix, but they are usually just sweetened strawberry-flavored liquid. Bars in tropical locations tend to bump it up a notch and stock better and meatier brands, but the very best is a blend of fresh crushed strawberries, fresh lime juice, and simple syrup to make a pourable strawberry mix. At home you can buy the frozen strawberries that are packed in sugar to help bulk up the mixture. Lime juice is an essential part of this drink and it's also why it's appropriate to garnish with a lime wedge.

White Lion

2 ounces light rum
¼ ounce raspberry liqueur
¾ ounce fresh lime juice

½ ounce simple syrup
½ ounce curaçao
berries and lime wedge

Combine all liquid ingredients and shake with ice. Strain into a white wine glass filled with crushed ice. Garnish with berries and a lime wedge.

A Bar Riddle

If Mackensey, Alex, Carly, Leslie, Meagan, and Charlie like Chocolate Martinis, and Pete, Samantha, Trinity, and Victoria do not, does Quinn like Chocolate Martinis? The answer: Quinn does not like Chocolate Martinis because only those with initials from A through M like Chocolate Martinis.

Wonderland Green Mint Tea

5 mint leaves
½ ounce simple syrup
2 lime wedges

1 ounce light rum
green tea to fill
1 tablespoon honey

In a mug, muddle the mint in simple syrup with the lime wedges. Add the rum. Pour steaming green tea on top. Sweeten with honey to taste.

Yellow Bird

2 ounces light rum
½ ounce banana liqueur

½ ounce Galliano
¾ ounce fresh lime juice

Combine all ingredients and shake with ice. Strain into a tall glass of ice.

☕ Zombie

1 ounce light rum   ½ ounce 151 float
1 ounce dark rum   bar punch mix to fill
1 ounce apricot brandy   orange slice and cherry

Combine all ingredients and shake with ice. Strain into a tall glass of ice. Garnish with an orange slice and cherry.

The Zombie

The Zombie was created by Donn Beach (born Ernest Raymond Beaumont Gantt), owner of the tiki-themed Don the Beachcomber Restaurant in Hollywood, California. The drink was served at the 1939 World's Fair in New York and was also known as the Tahitian Rum Punch.

Chapter 9

Tequila: Mexican Beauty

Tequila is North America's first distilled spirit. The name comes from a Mexican town of the same name in the state of Jalisco. Tequila is made from the hearts of the agave plant. By law, for a liquor to be called and labeled tequila, 51 percent of it must be made from the blue agave plant grown near the town of Tequila.

Tequila History

Legend has it that the Aztec ruler Montezuma welcomed the Spanish explorer Hernando Cortez with a wine made from the agave plant. Poor man. The ungrateful Cortez became Montezuma's conqueror, took the agave wine, and distilled it to make tequila. This all took place around the early 1500s, and by the 1600s tequila was being mass-produced. Jose Cuervo tequila was introduced in 1795.

Tequila Today

With its distinctive dry taste, tequila is the basis for marvelous drinks, not the least of which is the margarita. There are five types of tequila: blanco (not aged, and also called white or silver), joven (blanco that is colored to look gold), reposado (gold from aging), anejo (aged the longest in oak barrels where it acquires its mellow color of gold), and maduro (mature, vintage, or ultra aged). Maduro tequilas were first introduced in 2006. This tequila is aged a minimum of three years in oak barrels from France and Canada and produces a smooth, superior spirit that is often called the cognac of tequila.

Acapulco Clam Digger

1½ ounces blanco tequila
3 ounces tomato juice
3 ounces clam juice
1 tablespoon horseradish
¼ ounce fresh lemon juice
splash Worcestershire sauce
splash Tabasco
lemon wedge

Put liquid ingredients and horseradish into a highball glass. Stir and garnish with a lemon wedge.

Alamo

1 ounce aged tequila
1 ounce fresh orange juice

1 ounce pineapple juice
Sprite or 7-Up to fill

Pour the first three ingredients into a highball glass of ice. Fill with Sprite or 7-Up.

Alamo PowWow

1 ounce blanco tequila
1 ounce Hot Damn cinnamon schnapps

club soda to fill

Pour the tequila and schnapps into a highball glass of ice. Fill with club soda.

Anita Rita Now

1½ ounces blanco tequila
¾ ounce triple sec
½ ounce lime juice
3 ounces limeade

Pour the gold tequila in a shot glass. Pour the triple sec and the lime juice in another shot glass. Pour the limeade in a rocks glass. Then drink each one right after the other. That is the fastest Rita when you need a Rita now!

Aztec Gold

1 ounce aged tequila
½ ounce crème de banana
¼ ounce amaretto
½ ounce Galliano

Shake all ingredients with ice. Strain into a martini glass.

Beer Belly Margarita

kosher salt
1½ ounces blanco tequila
2 ounces Mexican beer

juice from a lime
2 ounces simple syrup
lime wheel

Rim a margarita glass with salt. Pour the tequila, Mexican beer, lime juice, and syrup in a blender with a cup of ice and blend. Pour into the glass and garnish with the lime wheel.

Between the Hotel Sheets Margarita

kosher salt
2 ounces aged tequila
1 ounce Grand Marnier

juice from a lime
1 ounce simple syrup
lime wheel

Rim a margarita glass with salt. Pour the tequila, Grand Marnier, lime juice, and syrup in a blender with a cup of ice and blend. Pour into the glass and garnish with the lime wheel.

Bird of Paradise

1 ounce tequila
1 ounce white crème do cacao

1 ounce amaretto
1 ounce cream

Shake all ingredients with ice. Strain into a martini glass.

Bloody Maria

2 ounces aged tequila
Bloody Mary mix to fill

celery and lime wedge

Pour the tequila into a tall glass of ice. Fill with Bloody Mary mix. Stir. Garnish with celery and a lime wedge.

Blue Voodoo Doll

1¼ ounces Voodoo Tiki Blue Dragon (Blue Kiwi) tequila
½ ounce blue curaçao
2 ounces sour mix
¼ ounce cranberry juice
sugar for rimming

Shake all liquid ingredients with ice. Strain into a sugar-rimmed martini glass.

Brave Bull

2 ounces blanco tequila   1 ounce coffee liqueur

Pour ingredients into an old-fashioned glass almost filled with ice. Stir well.

Cactus Bite

2 ounces aged tequila   2 ounces lemon juice
¼ ounce triple sec   ½ teaspoon sugar
¼ ounce Drambuie   dash bitters

Shake all ingredients with ice. Strain into a martini glass.

Charro Negro

1 ounce Herradura blanco tequila   cola to fill
juice of half a lemon

Pour the tequila and lemon juice into a highball glass of ice. Fill with cola.

Compadre

1½ ounces blanco tequila
½ teaspoon maraschino liqueur

1 teaspoon grenadine syrup
2 dashes orange bitters

Shake all ingredients with ice. Strain into a martini glass.

Cranberry Cosmorita

kosher salt
1½ ounces blanco tequila
½ ounce triple sec
juice from half a lime

2 ounces cranberry juice
2 ounces sweet-and-sour mix
lime wheel

Rim a margarita glass with salt. Blend all ingredients in a blender
with a cup of ice. Pour into the glass and garnish with lime.

Downsider

1½ ounces blanco tequila
½ ounce crème de banana
½ ounce Galliano

1 ounce cream
¼ ounce grenadine

Shake all ingredients with ice. Strain into a martini glass.

Dynamite

1 ounce reposado tequila
1 ounce blanco tequila
1 ounce Clamato juice
1 ounce fresh lime juice
¼ ounce Tabasco
kosher salt

Rim a short glass with kosher salt. Fill the glass with ice, and
pour all ingredients in.

El Diablo

2 ounces aged tequila
¾ ounce crème de cassis

ginger ale to fill
lime wedge

Pour the tequila and crème de cassis into a highball glass of ice. Fill with ginger ale. Garnish with lime wedge.

El Niño

¾ ounce aged tequila
¾ ounce Alizé Gold
¾ ounce grenadine

Prepare this layered drink in a rocks glass three-quarters full of ice, using a layering spoon on the rim of the glass. Pour slowly and carefully to prevent the layers from mixing. Pour the ingredients in the order they are listed.

Flat Tire at the Border

2 ounces blanco tequila
1 ounce black sambuca

Shake the tequila and sambuca over ice. Strain into a rocks glass of ice.

Freddy Fudpucker

1 ounce blanco tequila
½ ounce Galliano
orange juice

Pour the tequila into a highball glass filled with ice and fill with orange juice. Stir. Float the Galliano on top.

God Bless Texastini

1 ounce aged tequila
1 ounce Tequila Rose

1 ounce orange juice
1 ounce pineapple juice

Shake all ingredients with ice. Strain into a martini glass.

Green Iguana

kosher salt
1½ ounces aged tequila
1 ounce melon liqueur
3 ounces sweet-and-sour mix
lime wheel

Rim a margarita glass with salt. Pour the tequila, melon liqueur, and sweet-and-sour mix in a blender with a cup of ice and blend. Pour into the glass and garnish with the lime wheel.

Habla Español Fly

1½ ounces blanco tequila
1½ ounces coffee liqueur

2 ounces cold black coffee
cream to fill

Pour the tequila, coffee liqueur, and the cold coffee into a highball glass of ice, then fill with cream. Stir.

Horny Margarita

kosher salt
1½ ounces Sauza Hornitos reposado tequila
1 ounce Cointreau
juice of half a lime
3 ounces sweet-and-sour mix
lime wheel

Rim a margarita glass with salt. Pour the tequila, Cointreau, lime juice, and sweet-and-sour mix into a blender with a cup of ice and blend. Pour into the glass and garnish with the lime wheel.

A Texan Walks into an Irish Pub

A Texan walks into a pub in Ireland and says, "I hear you Irish are a bunch of hard drinkers, so I'll give $500 to anybody in here who can drink ten pints of Guinness back to back." No one takes the Texan up on his offer, and one man even leaves the pub. Thirty minutes later, the man who left reappears and tells Texan he'll take the offer. The Irishman downs all ten pints of Guinness. The Texan gives the Irishman the $500 and asks, "Where did you go for those thirty minutes?" The Irishman replies, "Oh, I had to go to the pub down the street to see if I could do it first."

Hypnotizing Margarita

kosher salt
1½ ounces aged tequila
1 ounce Hpnotiq

juice from half a lime
3 ounces sweet-and-sour mix
lime wheel

Rim a margarita glass with salt. Pour the tequila, Hpnotiq, lime juice, and sweet-and-sour mix in a blender with a cup of ice and blend. Pour into the glass and garnish with lime wheel.

Jalisco Smash

3 sprigs mint (one for garnish)
half a fresh peach, chopped
2 teaspoons sugar

1 ounce fresh lime juice
2 ounces aged tequila

Muddle 2 springs of mint, peach half, sugar, and lime juice in a mixer glass. Add the tequila. Shake in a shaker tin of ice. Strain over a short glass of crushed ice. Garnish with a mint sprig.

Jumping Beans

1½ ounces aged tequila
½ ounce sambuca

3 coffee beans

Pour the tequila and sambuca into a brandy snifter and drop in the coffee beans.

Key Lime Pie Margarita

1 crushed graham cracker
1½ ounces aged tequila
½ ounce key lime crème liqueur

3 ounces key lime yogurt
juice from half a lime
lime wheel

Rim a margarita glass with a crushed graham cracker. Put the remaining ingredients in a blender with a cup of ice and blend. Pour into the glass and garnish with a lime wheel.

Kiss from a Rosarita

kosher salt
1½ ounces aged tequila
1 ounce Tequila Rose

3 ounces sweet-and-sour mix
3 strawberries
lime wheel

Rim a margarita glass with salt. Put the liquid ingredients and the strawberries in a blender with a cup of ice and blend. Pour into the glass and garnish with a lime wheel.

Word Meanings
Agave comes from a Greek word that means "noble." *Tequila* means "the rock that cuts." Most believe the name originated from the sharp rocks created by lava that surround the town of Tequila.

La Bomba

1½ ounces blanco tequila
½ ounce Cointreau
1 ounce pineapple juice
1 ounce orange juice
¼ ounce grenadine

Combine and shake all ingredients with ice. Strain into a martini glass.

Lemon Raspberry Rita

1½ ounces aged tequila
½ ounce Chambord raspberry liqueur
juice from half a lemon
lemonade to fill
lemon wheel

Fill a margarita glass with ice. Pour the tequila, raspberry liqueur, and lemon juice into a shaker. Shake and starin into the mararita glass. Fill with lemonade. Garnish with a lemon wheel.

Lolita

2 ounces blanco tequila
1 banana, chopped (save half for a garnish)
1 mango, chopped (save half for a garnish)
1 papaya, chopped (save half for a garnish)
2 ounces orange juice

Blend the tequila, half the banana, half the mango, half the papaya, and orange juice in a blender with a cup of ice. Pour into a margarita glass, then sprinkle the chopped garnishes on top.

Margarita

kosher salt
1½ ounces aged tequila
½ ounce Cointreau

1 ounce freshly squeezed lime juice
½ ounce simple syrup
lime wedge or wheel garnish

Rim a margarita glass with salt. Add ice to the glass. In a shaker tin of ice, shake all ingredients and strain into the margarita glass. Garnish with a lime wedge or wheel.

Mexican Madras

1 ounce blanco tequila
1 ounce orange juice

3 ounces cranberry juice
¼ ounce lime juice

Combine all ingredients in a shaker half filled with ice. Shake well. Strain into a highball glass of ice.

Mexican Moonlight

1 ounce black tequila
1 ounce black vodka
1 ounce lime juice
1 ounce simple syrup

Combine and shake all ingredients with ice. Strain into a martini glass.

Muy Bonita Rita

crushed graham crackers
1½ ounces aged tequila
1½ ounces Licor 43
1 ounce sweet-and-sour mix
1 ounce cream
lime wheel

Rim a martini glass with crushed graham crackers. Shake the tequila, Licor 43, sweet-and-sour-mix, and cream with ice. Strain into the glass. Garnish with a lime wheel.

Montezuma

2 ounces blanco tequila   1 egg yolk
1 ounce Madeira

Blend all ingredients with half a cup of crushed ice in a blender on low speed. Pour into a champagne flute and serve.

Petroleo

1 serrano chile, halved lengthwise and seeded (wash hands
    and kitchen tools immediately after seeding to avoid irritation)
2 ounces aged tequila
1 ounce fresh lime juice
dash salt and pepper
splash Worcestershire sauce
splash Maggi seasoning sauce

Drop one of the chile halves into a rocks glass. Fill the glass with ice. Put the rest of the ingredients into a shaker of ice (including the remaining chile half) and shake. Strain over the rocks glass of ice.

Piñata

1½ ounces blanco tequila   citrus soda (such as Fresca) to fill
½ ounce blue curaçao   handful of multicolored gummy bears

Pour the tequila and curaçao into a tall glass of ice. Fill with citrus soda. Garnish with a handful of gummy bears on top.

Salma Hayek

2 ounces aged tequila   2 ounces pomegranate juice
½ ounce vanilla schnapps   sugar for rimming

Combine and shake all liquid ingredients with ice. Strain into a sugar-rimmed martini glass.

Selena

2 ounces aged tequila   1 ounce honey
1 ounce fresh lime juice   2 dashes Regans' orange bitters

Combine and shake all ingredients with ice. Strain into a martini glass.

Shady Lady

1 ounce blanco tequila   fresh pink grapefruit juice to fill
1 ounce melon liqueur

Pour the tequila and melon liqueur into a highball glass of ice. Fill with grapefruit juice.

Silk Stocking

2 ounces aged tequila   1 ounce crème de cacao
1 ounce Chambord   1 ounce cream

Combine and shake all ingredients with ice. Strain into a martini glass.

South of the Peachy Border Rita

kosher salt
1½ ounces blanco tequila
1 ounce peach schnapps

⅛ ounce grenadine
3 ounces sweet-and-sour mix
lime wheel

Rim a margarita glass with salt. Pour the ingredients into a blender with a cup of ice and blend. Pour into the glass and garnish with a lime wheel.

Spanish Moss

1 ounce blanco tequila
1 ounce coffee liqueur

1 ounce crème de menthe

Combine and shake all ingredients with ice. Strain into a rocks glass of ice.

Strawberry Mojitorita

half a lime, chopped
3 mint sprigs (one for a garnish)
4 large strawberries
   (one for a garnish)

1½ ounces blanco tequila
½ ounce triple sec
1 ounce fresh lime juice
1 ounce simple syrup

Muddle the lime, two mint sprigs, and three strawberries in a shaker. Add the rest of the ingredients and ice. Shake and strain into a margarita glass of ice. Garnish.

Sunbathing on a Mexican Beach

1 ounce blanco tequila
1 ounce coconut rum
pineapple juice to fill

Pour the tequila and coconut rum into a tall glass of ice. Fill with pineapple juice.

Swim-Up Bar Margarita

kosher salt
1½ ounces blanco tequila
1 ounce blue curaçao

juice from half a lime
3 ounces sweet-and-sour mix
lime wheel

Rim a margarita glass with salt. Pour all ingredients in a blender with a cup of ice and blend. Pour into the glass and garnish with lime wheel.

Tasting Away in Margaritaville

kosher salt
1½ ounces blanco tequila
½ ounce triple sec

2 ounces mango nectar
1 ounce sweet-and-sour mix
lime wheel

Rim a margarita glass with salt. Pour the liquid ingredients into a blender with a cup of ice and blend. Pour into the glass and garnish with a lime wheel.

Tequila Mockingbird Margarita

kosher salt
1½ ounces aged tequila
½ ounce green crème de menthe

juice from half a lime
3 ounces sweet-and-sour mix
lime wheel

Rim a margarita glass with salt. Pour the liquid ingredients into a blender with a cup of ice and blend. Pour into the glass and garnish with a lime wheel.

Tequila Sunrise

1½ ounces blanco tequila
½ ounce grenadine

fresh orange juice to fill

Pour the tequila and grenadine into a highball glass of ice. Fill with fresh orange juice.

Tequila Sunrise Margarita

kosher salt
1½ ounces blanco tequila
½ ounce triple sec
½ ounce grenadine

1 ounce orange juice
1 ounce sweet-and-sour mix
lime wheel

Rim a margarita glass with salt. Pour liquid ingredients into a blender with a cup of ice and blend. Pour into the glass and garnish with a lime wheel.

The Tequila Sunrise

The Tequila Sunrise was created in Mexico in 1950s to welcome tourists to Acapulco and Cancun. The drink gained popularity again in the 1970s.

Tezón Caramel Apple Pie

1½ ounces Tezón tequila
½ ounce butterscotch schnapps
1 ounce apple cider
½ ounce fresh lemon juice

Shake all ingredients with ice. Strain into a martini glass.

Thorny Mexican

1 ounce aged tequila
2 ounces Tequila Rose crème liqueur
rose petal

Shake all liquid ingredients with ice, then strain into a martini glass. Garnish by dropping a rose petal on top.

Toreador

2 ounces blanco tequila
1 ounce crème de cacao
1 ounce cream
¼ teaspoon cocoa powder

Shake all ingredients with ice. Strain into a martini glass.

Jose Antonio Cuervo

In 1758, Jose Antonio Cuervo founded a distillery in the village of Tequila. Thirty-seven years later, his son Jose Guadalupe was granted the first license by the king of Spain to produce what was then called "wine of the earth."

White Sangriarita

kosher salt
1½ ounces blanco tequila
1 ounce white wine
4 ounces sweet-and-sour mix
lime wheel, orange wheel, lemon wheel, and cherry

Rim a margarita glass with salt. Pour the tequila, white wine, and sweet-and-sour mix into a blender with a cup of ice and blend. Pour into the glass and float the citrus wheels and cherry on top.

Chapter 10

Whiskey: Amber Waves of Grain

Four prominent countries—Scotland, Ireland, Canada, and the United States—produce whiskey, an alcohol distilled from fermented barley and other grains. Ireland and Scotland still argue over who made it first. Ireland and the United States spell whiskey with an "e," while Canada and Scotland do not. Each country makes different types of whiskey.

Types of Whiskey

Whiskeys from different regions have strikingly different tastes. Local grains go through an arduous process of distillation, fermentation, blending, and aging. Each whiskey region has its own techniques and traditions, which accounts for the vast difference in taste between Johnnie Walker and Jack Daniels.

Scotland produces blended Scotch whisky and single malt whisky. For a bottle to bear the "Scotch" label, it must be made in Scotland. The single malt is made from a single distillation of malted barley, while the blended contains a combination of single malts and grain whiskies.

Ireland produces Irish whiskey, and there are only three distilleries in the whole country. Irish whiskey comes in three types—pure pot still whiskey, single malt whiskey, and blended whiskey.

Canada produces blended whisky and rye whisky. Blended versions may combine many whiskies together to create a smooth-tasting final product.

America produces bourbon whiskey, corn whiskey, rye whiskey, blended whiskey, and Tennessee whiskey. High-end bourbon breaks down into two other categories called small batch bourbon and single barrel bourbon. By law, bourbon can only be made in America and a label can only say Kentucky bourbon if it's made in Kentucky.

Scotch

The different and distinctive tastes of Scotches are caused by the air quality, peat bogs, and water where the liquor is made, a fact that should make ardent environmentalists out of all Scotch drinkers. There are eight regions of single malt producers in Scotland, and the product of each is unique. Admirers of single malts are usually devotees of a particular brand. Enthusiasts of a blended label maintain that the art is in the blending. But few would deny the supremacy of Scotch in the domain of whisky.

Affinity

2 ounces blended Scotch whisky
1 ounce sweet vermouth
1 ounce dry vermouth
3 dashes bitters

Pour ingredients into a shaker with ice. Shake and strain into a cocktail glass.

Aggravation

2 ounces blended Scotch whisky
1 ounce coffee liqueur

Pour both ingredients into a short glass of ice and stir.

Balmoral

2 ounces blended Scotch whisky   ½ ounce dry vermouth
½ ounce sweet vermouth   2 dashes bitters

Combine all ingredients in a mixing glass half filled with ice. Stir and strain into a cocktail glass.

⅄ Blue Blazer

¼ ounce simple syrup	1½ ounces boiling water
lemon twist	½ ounce blended Scotch whisky

You will be pouring hot flaming Scotch back and forth (chemistry-set style) so you'll need two mugs with handles that won't get hot. Some bartenders use silver plated or metal mugs to stay authentic to the original recipe in the 1800s. Fill both mugs with hot water and let them warm up while you boil the water. Further prep by putting the simple syrup and lemon twist into an Irish coffee mug. When the water boils, dump the hot water out of the mugs. Pour the Scotch and 1½ ounces of boiling water into *one* of the mugs and ignite with a match. Carefully pour the liquid stream of fire into the other mug and back again three or four times. Pour the drink into the Irish coffee mug.

The Blue Blazer

The Blue Blazer was created by the first celebrity bartender, Jerry Thomas. He traveled the world with a set of solid silver bar tools. Thomas published *How to Mix Drinks, or The Bon-Vivant's Companion,* in 1862 and followed that in 1887 with the first bartender guide, *The Bar-Tender's Guide or How to Mix All Kinds of Plain and Fancy Drinks*.

Blinder

2 ounces blended Scotch whisky	1 teaspoon grenadine
5 ounces grapefruit juice	

Pour Scotch and grapefruit juice into an ice-filled highball glass. Add grenadine and stir slightly.

Bobby Burns

1½ ounces blended Scotch whisky   1 teaspoon Bénédictine
1½ ounces sweet vermouth

Pour ingredients into a mixing glass nearly filled with ice. Stir and strain into a cocktail glass.

Godfather

2 ounces blended Scotch whisky   ¾ ounce amaretto

Pour Scotch and amaretto into an old-fashioned glass over ice.

Modern Cocktail

1½ ounces blended Scotch whisky   ½ teaspoon lemon juice
1 teaspoon dark rum   2 dashes orange bitters
½ teaspoon anisette

Pour all ingredients into a shaker half filled with ice. Shake well and strain into a cocktail glass.

Perfect Rob Roy

2 ounces blended Scotch whisky   1 teaspoon dry vermouth
1 teaspoon sweet vermouth   lemon twist

Pour liquid ingredients into a mixing glass nearly filled with ice. Stir and strain into a cocktail glass. Garnish with lemon.

Perfect
Traditionally, whenever a cocktail recipe is prefaced with the word "perfect," the drink includes both dry and sweet vermouth.

Rob Roy

1½ ounces blended Scotch whisky   dash orange bitters
½ ounce sweet vermouth   lemon twist

Combine the liquid ingredients in a mixing glass. Stir well.
Strain into a cocktail glass. Garnish with lemon twist.

Rusty Nail

1½ ounces Scotch   ½ ounce Drambuie

Pour ingredients into a short glass of ice.

Scotch and Milk

2 ounces blended Scotch whisky   milk to fill

Pour ingredients into a short glass of ice.

Scotch and Soda

2 ounces blended Scotch whisky   club soda to fill

Pour ingredients into a short glass of ice.

Scotch Holiday Sour

1½ ounces blended Scotch whisky   ½ ounce sweet vermouth
1 ounce cherry brandy   1 ounce lemon juice

Combine ingredients in a shaker half filled with ice. Shake
well. Strain into a short glass of ice.

Scotch Mist

2 ounces blended Scotch whisky   crushed ice

Pour Scotch into a short glass of crushed ice.

⧓ Scotch on the Rocks

2 ounces blended Scotch whisky

Pour Scotch into a short glass of ice.

⧓ Scotch Sour

1½ ounces blended Scotch whisky
1 ounce lemon juice

Combine ingredients in a shaker half filled with ice. Shake well. Strain into a short glass of ice.

Ireland: Whiskey in the Jar

Irish whiskey comes in several forms. There is a single malt whiskey made from 100 percent malted barley distilled in a pot still, and a grain whiskey made from grains distilled in a column still. Grain whiskey is much lighter and more neutral in flavor than single malt whiskey and is almost never bottled as a single grain. It is instead used to blend with single malts to produce a lighter blended whiskey. Unique to Irish whiskey is pure pot still whiskey (100 percent barley, both malted and unmalted, distilled in a pot still). The "green" unmalted barley gives pure pot still whiskey a spicy, uniquely Irish quality. Like single malt, pure pot still is sold alone or blended with grain whiskey. Usually no real distinction is made between blended whiskeys made from single malt or pure pot still.

Black Thorn

1 ounce Irish whiskey
1 ounce dry vermouth

3 dashes Pernod
3 dashes bitters

Pour ingredients into a shaker with ice. Stir and strain into a short glass of ice.

Blarney Stone

2 ounces Irish whiskey
½ teaspoon anisette
½ teaspoon Cointreau

½ teaspoon maraschino syrup
dash bitters

Pour all ingredients into a short glass of ice and stir.

Irish Car Bomb

½ ounce Irish whiskey
½ ounce Irish cream

8 ounces Guinness Stout

Pour the Irish whiskey and Irish cream into a shot glass. Drop it into a glass of Guinness. Chug before the drink curdles.

Irish Coffee

coffee to fill
1½ ounces Irish whiskey

1 teaspoon brown sugar
whipped cream

Preheat an Irish coffee mug with hot water. Pour out the water and add coffee until the mug is three-quarters full. Add the whiskey and sugar and stir. Fill to the top with whipped cream.

Irish Coffee Cake

Add some kick to a brunch staple by soaking a coffee cake in a syrup made of Irish whiskey, coffee, and sugar.

Irish Magic

1 ounce Irish whiskey
¼ ounce white crème de cacao

5 ounces orange juice

Pour all ingredients over ice in a tall glass and stir.

Irish Rickey

1½ ounces Irish whiskey
juice of half a lime

club soda

Pour the Irish whiskey and lime juice into a highball glass of ice. Top with club soda.

Irish Shillelagh

1½ ounces Irish whiskey
juice of half a lemon
1 teaspoon powdered sugar

1 tablespoon sloe gin
1 tablespoon light rum

Combine all ingredients in a shaker with ice. Shake and strain into a short glass of ice.

Paddy Cocktail

2 ounces Irish whiskey
several dashes angostura bitters
¾ ounce sweet vermouth

Pour all ingredients into a short glass of ice and stir.

Shamrock

1½ ounces Irish whiskey
¾ ounce dry vermouth

1 teaspoon green Chartreuse
1 teaspoon green crème de menthe

Pour all ingredients into a short glass of ice and stir.

North American Whiskey/Whisky

It's no surprise that the Mint Julep and bourbon have the same home territory—Bourbon County, Kentucky. Bourbon whiskey, born in the late 1700s, is America's original native brew. Like most liquors, its ingredients are humble—corn and wood. But bourbon's distinctive flavor emerges from its 51 percent corn mash and the charred oak barrels in which the liquor ages. A "mash," the source of all whiskies and beers, is milled cereal cooked in water. The quality of that water is all-important. Eighty percent of the world's bourbon is produced in America because of the clear limestone spring water of the Kentucky hills. People think that Jack Daniel's Tennessee whiskey gets its flavor from being a sour mash. Wrong! Many whiskeys are made from a sour mash. JD gets its flavor from dripping through ten feet of sugar maple charcoal before it's put into charred barrels.

Canadian whisky production grew tremendously due to the American Prohibition. Windsor, Ontario, supplied its upriver neighbors in Detroit, Michigan, with alcohol, and the porous U.S. Canadian border allowed for a steady trade between the two countries. Today, the most popular Canadian whiskies are Crown Royal, Canadian Club, Seagram's V.O., and Black Velvet.

Ace of Spades

1 ounce Crown Royal Canadian whisky
1 ounce amaretto
cola to fill

Pour Crown Royal and amaretto into a highball glass of ice. Fill with cola.

Agent Orange

1 ounce Tennessee whiskey
1 ounce Southern Comfort

orange juice to fill

Pour the whiskey and Southern Comfort into a highball glass of ice. Fill with orange juice.

Algonquin

1½ ounces rye whiskey
1 ounce dry vermouth

1 ounce pineapple juice

Combine ingredients in a shaker half filled with ice. Shake well. Strain into a short glass of ice.

All American

1 ounce bourbon
1 ounce Southern Comfort
2 ounces cola

Pour all ingredients in an old-fashioned glass and stir.

Americana

1 ounce Tennessee whiskey
1 teaspoon fine sugar
dash bitters
chilled champagne to fill

Pour the first three ingredients into a champagne glass. Fill with champagne.

Kentucky Whisky

America spells whiskey with the "e." However, Kentucky spells it without the "e." This is because Kentucky whisky is made Scottish style using cold winter wheat instead of the summer wheat. By doing this, Kentucky honors the Scottish ways and uses the Scottish spelling as well.

American Cobbler

1 ounce bourbon
1 ounce Southern Comfort
¼ ounce peach brandy
4 dashes lemon juice

simple syrup (to taste)
club soda to fill
peach slice and mint leaf (optional)

Pour the first five ingredients into an ice-filled shaker. Shake and strain into a highball glass of ice. Fill with club soda. Garnish with peach slice and mint leaf if you want.

Bourbon and Branch

2 ounces bourbon   still mineral water to fill

Pour the bourbon into a short glass of ice. Fill with water.

Bourbon Daisy

1½ ounces bourbon
½ ounce lemon juice
1 teaspoon grenadine

club soda to fill
¼ ounce Southern Comfort
orange slice and pineapple stick

Shake the bourbon, lemon juice, and grenadine with ice. Strain into a highball glass of ice. Fill with club soda and float the Southern Comfort. Garnish with the orange slice and pineapple stick.

Bourbon on the Rocks

2 ounces bourbon

Pour bourbon into a short glass of ice and stir.

Bourbon Satin

2 ounces bourbon
1 ounce white crème de menthe
1 ounce light cream

Combine ingredients in a shaker half filled with ice. Shake, then strain into a cocktail glass.

Bull and Bear

2 ounces bourbon
1 ounce orange curaçao
¼ ounce grenadine
1 ounce lime juice
1 cherry

Combine liquid ingredients in a shaker half filled with ice. Shake and strain into a cocktail glass. Garnish with a cherry.

Elijah Craig

Elijah Craig, a Baptist preacher, invented bourbon whiskey. He was also the first to discover that aging whiskey in charred barrels changed the flavor and color. The only barrels he could afford in the beginning were used herring barrels, so he'd torch the insides to burn the fish smell out of them. Today, all whiskey factories char their oak barrels.

California Lemonade

2 ounces blended whiskey
1 tablespoon sugar
1 ounce lemon juice

1 ounce lime juice
club soda to fill
lemon wedge

Pour the first four ingredients into a shaker half filled with ice. Shake well. Strain into a highball glass of ice. Fill with club soda and garnish with a lemon wedge.

Canadian Cherry

2 ounces Canadian whisky
½ ounce cherry-flavored brandy
1 teaspoon lemon juice

2 teaspoons orange juice
cherry

Shake liquid ingredients in a shaker half filled with ice. Strain into a highball glass of ice. Garnish with a cherry.

Canadian Cocktail

1½ ounces Canadian whisky
½ ounce Cointreau

1 teaspoon sugar
dash bitters

Combine ingredients in a shaker half filled with ice. Shake, then strain into a cocktail glass.

Gentleman's Cocktail

2 ounces bourbon
½ ounce crème de menthe
½ ounce brandy

club soda to fill
lemon twist

Pour liquors into a highball glass of ice. Fill with club soda. Garnish with a lemon twist.

Jack Be Nimble Java

1 ounce Jack Daniel's
1 ounce amaretto

hot coffee to fill
whipped cream (optional)

Pour Jack Daniel's and amaretto into a mug. Fill with coffee.

☆ John Collins

2 ounces rye whiskey
juice of half a lemon
½ ounce simple syrup

club soda to fill
orange slice and cherry

Shake the first three ingredients. Strain into a Collins glass of ice. Fill with club soda and garnish with an orange and cherry.

J. R.'s Godfather

2 ounces bourbon   ½ ounce amaretto

Pour bourbon and amaretto into a short glass of ice. Stir well.

> "How well I remember my first encounter with the Devil's Brew. I happened to stumble across a case of bourbon— and went right on stumbling for several days thereafter."
> —actor and comedian W. C. Fields

Kentucky Colonel

1½ ounces bourbon
½ ounce Bénédictine

lemon twist

Combine ingredients in a mixing glass half filled with ice. Stir, then strain into a cocktail glass. Serve with a lemon twist.

Lady's Cocktail

2 ounces blended whiskey
½ ounce anisette

dash bitters

Add to a shaker half filled with ice; shake and strain.

Lynchburg Lemonade

1½ ounces Jack Daniel's
½ ounce triple sec
2 ounces sweet-and-sour mix

Sprite or 7-Up to fill
lemon wedge

Pour the first three ingredients into a tall glass of ice. Fill with Sprite or 7-Up. Garnish with a lemon wedge.

Manhattan

2 ounces rye whiskey
½ ounce sweet vermouth

2 dashes angostura bitters
cherry

Pour liquid ingredients into a shaker. Shake and strain into a cocktail glass. Garnish with a cherry. Manhattans can also be served on the rocks.

Manhattan

It is believed that a bartender at a party hosted by Winston Churchill's mother invented the Manhattan. The party was at the Manhattan Club in New York City.

Man O' War

2 ounces bourbon
1 ounce orange curaçao
½ ounce sweet vermouth
juice of ½ lime

Shake all ingredients. Strain into a cocktail glass.

Millionaire

2 ounces rye bourbon
1 ounce orange curaçao
1 teaspoon grenadine
1 teaspoon framboise
white of 1 egg

Shake all ingredients. Strain into a cocktail glass.

Y Mint Julep

5 sprigs of spearmint leaves
2 ounces bourbon
1 tablespoon sugar

Muddle 4 spearmint sprigs and the sugar in a highball glass. Fill with ice. Add the bourbon and stir until glass gets very cold. Add more ice if needed. Garnish with remaining sprig.

The Mint Julep
The Mint Julep is the official drink of the Kentucky Derby. The mint should be infused with the bourbon and served in a traditional silver cup. The cocktail should be stirred until frost forms on the outside of the cup.

Seven and Seven

2 ounces Seagram's 7   Sprite or 7-Up to fill

Pour liquor into a highball glass of ice. Fill with Sprite or 7-Up.

 Old-Fashioned

1 tablespoon sugar   2 dashes angostura bitters
1 orange slice   2 ounces rye, bourbon, or whiskey
I cherry

Muddle the sugar, orange slice, cherry, and bitters in an old-fashioned glass with ice. Fill with ice. Add the whiskey.

> **Original Old-Fashioned**
> The original Old-Fashioned is built with a spoon of sugar, two dashes of bitters, a spoon of water, ice, rye whiskey, and a lemon peel garnish. Adding club soda or water is incorrect.

Old Pal

1 ounce Canadian whisky   1 ounce Campari
1 ounce dry vermouth

Pour ingredients into a short glass of ice and stir.

The Queen Stinger

2 ounces Crown Royal Canadian whisky
1 ounce white crème de menthe

Pour the Crown Royal and the white crème de menthe into a short glass of ice and stir.

🍸 Rye and Ginger

2 ounces rye whiskey　　　　　　ginger ale to fill

Pour rye into a highball glass of ice and fill with ginger ale. Stir.

🍸 Sazerac

½ teaspoon absinthe substitute　　2 ounces rye whiskey, chilled
1 dash Peychaud's bitters　　　　lemon peel
½ teaspoon simple syrup

Fill an old-fashioned glass with ice to chill the glass. Dump the ice out and coat the glass with absinthe substitute by swirling it around. Pour out most of what remains. Add the bitters, simple syrup, and chilled rye. Twist a lemon peel and run it around the rim of the glass, colored side out, then discard peel.

The Sazerac
This is one of the first cocktails on record. It was invented in New Orleans by Antoine Amadie Peychaud (pay-SHOWD). He was a pharmacist from the West Indies who also invented Peychaud's bitters.

Southern Lady

2 ounces bourbon　　　　　　　3 ounces pineapple juice
1 ounce Southern Comfort　　　　Sprite or 7-Up to fill
1 ounce amaretto

Pour the first four ingredients into a tall glass of ice. Fill with Sprite or 7-Up.

T-Bird

1½ ounces Canadian whisky
½ ounce amaretto

2 ounces pineapple juice
1 ounce orange juice

Pour all ingredients into a tall glass of ice. Stir.

SoCo

Many believe that Southern Comfort (Cuff and Buttons was its first name) is a whiskey-based liqueur. While it is a liqueur, it does not have whiskey in it. It's made from crushed peaches, apricots, and honey with a neutral grain spirit base.

Ward 8

1½ ounces bourbon
½ ounce lemon juice

½ ounce orange juice
1 teaspoon grenadine

Shake all ingredients with ice. Strain into a cocktail glass.

Whiskey Sour

2 ounces bourbon or whiskey
1 ounce lemon juice
1 ounce simple syrup

Shake all ingredients, then strain into a short glass of ice.

Chapter 11

Shots and Shooters

Shots and shooters are meant to be drunk very quickly in one gulp. They can measure from 1 ounce up to almost 4 ounces and are served in shot glasses, cordial glasses, shooter glasses, or rocks glasses. The difference between a shot and a shooter is based on the alcohol content. For example, a shot of tequila and a Liquid Cocaine are both pure alcohol, so they are shots. A Purple Hooter and a Red Snapper have a nonalcoholic mix to them, so they are shooters.

191

Shot History

A classic image of downing shots comes from old western movies when a cowboy would stroll into the local saloon. Things were simple—just beer and shots. Ancient diggings reveal that shots have been around a lot longer then that. In 1982, a Tang Dynasty (618–907 CE) vessel used for drinking games was unearthed in Dantu county in Jiangsu province. It has a tortoise-shaped pedestal and a barrel to hold liquor. It's inscribed with a quotation from the Analects of Confucius—an instruction to drink, persuade others to drink, punish, or let go. It's believed to be a drinking game relic.

Types of Shots and Shooters

Shots and shooters can be prepared one of three ways: neat, layered, and chilled straight up. Types and names for shots and shooters can be shot, shooter, drop, bomb, and slammer. Drops and bombs refer to a shot of something being dropped into a glass of something else and then chugged. A slammer is slammed down on the table, and you drink it while it fizzes. Shots and shooters can also be layered or flamed (both of which are exactly what they sound like).

Know that you can take practically any popular drink and make a shooter from it by reducing the amount of mixer. When ordering shooters at a club, you really want to watch the bartender make them because you can get ripped off. I've seen bartenders only put 1 ounce of alcohol for six shooters, filling it up with mixer to make it look like they are giving you a large shooter.

Shots

Shots are 100 percent alcohol. There are many sizes of shot glasses, so adjust the amounts to fit your glassware.

❤ Alabama Slammer Shot

⅓ ounce Southern Comfort   ⅓ ounce sloe gin
⅓ ounce amaretto

Shake and strain into a shot glass.

Banana Jack

¾ ounce Jack Daniel's   ¾ ounce banana liqueur

Shake and strain into a shot glass.

Bazooka Joe

⅓ ounce Irish cream   ⅓ ounce banana liqueur
⅓ ounce blue curaçao

Shake and strain into a shot glass.

Beam Me Up, Scotty

½ ounce coffee liqueur   ½ ounce Irish cream
½ ounce crème de banana

Shake and strain into a shot glass.

Black Death

½ ounce black vodka   ½ ounce Jägermeister
½ ounce black sambuca

Shake and strain into a shot glass.

Homemade Shot Glasses of Ice

You'll need small Dixie cups, snow cone cups, and duct tape. Strengthen the tips of the snow cone cups with duct tape. Fill the Dixie cups three-quarters full with water; then stick the snow cone cups in, point side down, until the water level reaches the top. Duct-tape the cups in place and freeze. Rip off the duct tape and cups, and you'll have ice shot glasses.

Blue Balls

½ ounce blue curaçao
½ ounce coconut rum

½ ounce peach schnapps
squeeze of a lemon wedge

Shake and strain into a shot glass.

Brain Hemorrhage

1 ounce peach schnapps
¼ ounce Irish cream

¼ ounce grenadine syrup

First, pour the peach schnapps into a shot glass. Slowly add the Irish cream, and it will clump and settle at the bottom. Next, slowly pour grenadine to give it a bloody, disgusting brain-hemorrhage look.

Chocolate Cake

½ ounce citrus vodka
½ ounce Frangelico

lemon wedge

Shake and strain the vodka and Frangelico into a shot glass. Drink the shot, then bite into the lemon. For some reason, it will taste like chocolate cake.

❦ Jelly Bean

½ ounce blackberry brandy ½ ounce anisette or sambuca

Shake and strain into a shot glass.

❦ Lemon Drop Shot

1½ ounces citrus vodka sugar for rimming

Shake and strain into a sugar-rimmed shot glass.

❦ Liquid Cocaine

⅓ ounce Jägermeister ⅓ ounce Rumple Minze
⅓ ounce Goldschläger

Shake and strain into a shot glass if ingredients are room temperature. If liqueur is already chilled, just pour into a shot glass.

Oatmeal Cookie

Kahlúa Goldschläger
Bailey's

Shake equal parts of each alcohol and strain into a shot glass.

❦ Peanut Butter and Jelly

¾ ounce Frangelico ¾ ounce Chambord

Shake and strain into a shot glass.

Polar Bear

½ ounce white crème de cacao
½ ounce peppermint schnapps

Shake and strain into a shot glass.

Prairie Fire Shooter

1½ ounces tequila   3 dashes Tabasco

Pour tequila into a shot glass and add the Tabasco.

Russian Quaalude

⅓ ounce vodka   ⅓ ounce Frangelico
⅓ ounce Irish cream

Shake and strain into a shot glass.

Homemade Shot Glasses of Chocolate

You'll need baking chocolate, a double boiler or mock double boiler, two-ounce plastic cups and one-ounce plastic cups (found in restaurant supply stores), unflavored cooking spray (like PAM), and a cooking sheet. Melt the chocolate in the double boiler. Spray the *insides* of the two-ounce portion cups and the *outsides* of the one-ounce portion cups with the cooking spray to prevent sticking. Pour chocolate three-quarters of the way up the two-ounce cups, then place the one-ounce cups inside until the chocolate oozes up to the top. This molds the shot glass. Place on a cooking sheet and put in the freezer for about ten minutes to set up. Remove from the freezer and pop off the portion cups.

Sammy Jäger

1 ounce sambuca
1 ounce Jägermeister

Shake and strain into a shot glass.

Three Wise Men

½ ounce Johnnie Walker Scotch whisky
½ ounce Jim Beam bourbon whiskey
½ ounce Jack Daniel's Tennessee whiskey

Shake and strain into a shot glass.

Three Wise Men Go Hunting

½ ounce Johnnie Walker Scotch whisky
½ ounce Jim Beam bourbon whiskey
½ ounce Jack Daniel's Tennessee whiskey
½ ounce Wild Turkey bourbon whiskey

Shake and strain into a shot glass.

Three Wise Men Visit Mexico

½ ounce Johnnie Walker Scotch whisky
½ ounce Jim Beam bourbon whiskey
½ ounce Jack Daniel's Tennessee whiskey
½ ounce Jose Cuervo gold tequila

Shake and strain into a shot glass.

Shooters

Shooters have a mix to them, so you need a larger glass,
shooter glass, or rocks glass to hold them.

Blue Marlin Shooter

1 ounce light rum
½ ounce blue curaçao
1 ounce lime juice

Pour ingredients into a mixing glass half filled with ice. Stir. Strain into a large shot, shooter, or rocks glass.

Broken Down Golf Cart

¾ ounce melon liqueur   ¼ ounce cranberry juice
¾ ounce amaretto   ¼ ounce lime juice

Shake and strain into a large shot, shooter, or rocks glass.

Cement Mixer

1½ ounces Irish cream   ¼ ounce Rose's lime juice

This is a gag shot. Pour the ingredients into a shot glass and drink. It curdles in your mouth.

Kamikaze

1½ ounces vodka   ¼ ounce lime juice
½ ounce triple sec

Shake and strain into a large shot, shooter, or rocks glass.

Shooters of Yesterday
Today anything poured into a martini glass is called a Martini. Just know that the chugged shooters of yesterday are really just the flavored Martinis you sip today. A real Martini is gin and dry vermouth. Period.

Lemon Drop Shooter

sugar for rimming
½ ounce triple sec
1½ ounces lemon vodka
1 ounce sweet-and-sour mix

Rim a shooter or rocks glass with sugar. Shake and strain ingredients into a glass.

Quarter and Shot Glass Trick

Set a glass on top of a bill. Then balance a coin on the rim of the glass. The challenge is to get the bill out from underneath the glass without jerking it quickly or shimmying it around. The answer? Roll the bill and it will push the glass off.

Mind Eraser

1 ounce vodka
1 ounce coffee liqueur
club soda to fill

Pour the ingredients into a short glass of ice. Fill with club soda. Stick in a straw and suck all at once.

Monkey's Lunch

1 ounce banana liqueur
1 ounce coffee liqueur
1 ounce milk or cream

Shake and strain into a large shot, shooter, or rocks glass.

Orgasm Shooter

⅓ ounce amaretto
⅓ ounce coffee liqueur
⅓ ounce Irish cream

Shake and strain into a large shot, shooter, or rocks glass.

Purple Hooter

1½ ounces vodka
1 ounce raspberry liqueur

1 ounce pineapple juice
1 ounce sweet-and-sour mix

Shake and strain into a large shot, shooter, or rocks glass.

Raspberry Lemon Drop

sugar for rimming
1½ ounces raspberry vodka

½ ounce triple sec
1 ounce sweet-and-sour mix

Rim a rocks glass with sugar. Shake and strain into the glass.

Jell-O Shots
To make Jell-O shots, simply replace the cold water portion of a Jell-O recipe with alcohol. Use small plastic cups (one- to two-ounce cups) found at bulk restaurant supply stores or online. You can also buy lids to make them portable. The paper cups are sometimes called nut cups.

Redheaded Slut

1 ounce Jägermeister
1 ounce peach schnapps

2 ounces cranberry juice

Shake and strain into a large shot, shooter, or rocks glass.

Red Snapper

1 ounce Crown Royal
1 ounce amaretto

2 ounces cranberry juice

Shake and strain into a large shot, shooter, or rocks glass.

⅄ Screaming Orgasm

¼ ounce vodka
¼ ounce amaretto
¼ ounce coffee liqueur
¼ ounce Irish cream

Shake and strain into a large shot, shooter, or rocks glass.

Sexy Alligator

1 ounce melon liqueur
1 ounce amaretto
½ ounce Jägermeister
1 ounce pineapple juice

Shake and strain into a large shot, shooter, or rocks glass.

⅄ Snake Bite

2 ounces Yukon Jack
½ ounce Rose's lime juice

Shake and strain into a large shot, shooter, or rocks glass.

⅄ Snowshoe

¾ ounce Wild Turkey
¾ ounce peppermint schnapps

Shake and strain into a large shot, shooter, or rocks glass.

⅄ SoCo and Lime

2 ounces Southern Comfort
½ ounce Rose's lime juice

Shake and strain into a large shot, shooter, or rocks glass.

Stop Light

3 shots vodka
splash melon liqueur

splash orange juice
splash cranberry juice

Line up three shot glasses and pour 1 shot of vodka into each glass. Add a splash of melon liqueur to one, a splash of orange juice to another, and a splash of cranberry juice to the third. Drink them down red, yellow, green.

Surfer on Acid

1 ounce Jägermeister
1 ounce coconut rum

2 ounces pineapple juice

Shake and strain into a large shot, shooter, or rocks glass.

Tequila Slammer

1½ ounces tequila

2 ounces Sprite or 7-Up

Pour the ingredients into a rocks glass, place a napkin over the glass, and slam glass on the table or bar top so that it fizzes. Drink.

Tootsie Roll Shooter

1 ounce coffee liqueur
1 ounce crème de cacao

1 ounce orange juice

Shake and strain into a large shot, shooter, or rocks glass.

Washington Apple

1 ounce Crown Royal
1 ounce sour apple schnapps

1 ounce cranberry juice

Shake and strain into a large shot, shooter, or rocks glass.

> **Shooter Pyramid**
>
> Why not make a shooter pyramid out of six shooters?
> Three glasses will be on the bottom, two balanced on
> top of the space between those, and then one on top.
> You have to curve the pattern in order to strain into all
> the glasses.

Woo Woo

1 ounce vodka   1 ounce cranberry juice
1 ounce peach schnapps

Shake and strain into a large shot, shooter, or rocks glass.

Layered Shots

Liqueurs have different densities, so it's possible to *care-fully* layer them to create a rainbow or striped effect. The official name for this technique is *pousse-café*.

Astro Pop

¼ ounce grenadine   ¼ ounce melon liqueur
¼ ounce crème de banana   ¼ ounce vodka

Into a shot glass, layer each ingredient in order with a spoon.

B-52

½ ounce coffee liqueur   ½ ounce Grand Marnier
½ ounce Irish cream

Into a shot glass, layer each ingredient in order with a spoon.

Black Rose

¾ ounce Tequila Rose   ¾ ounce black vodka

Into a shot glass, layer each ingredient in order with a spoon.

Black Slippery Nipple

¾ ounce black sambuca   ¾ ounce Irish cream

Into a shot glass, layer each ingredient in order with a spoon.

Blow Job

½ ounce coffee liqueur   whipped cream
½ ounce Irish cream

Into a shot glass, layer the coffee liqueur and the Irish cream
in that order with a spoon. Top with whipped cream. The novelty of this shot is that the drinker sucks up the whipped cream
and then wraps his mouth around the glass and drinks with his
hands behind his back.

Buttery Nipple

½ ounce butterscotch schnapps   ½ ounce Irish cream

Into a shot glass, layer each ingredient in order with a spoon.

Candy Corn

⅓ ounce Galliano   ⅓ ounce cream
⅓ ounce orange curaçao

Into a shot glass, layer each ingredient in order with a spoon.

Captain's Stripes

¼ ounce coffee liqueur
¼ ounce Galliano

¼ ounce Irish cream
¼ ounce Captain Morgan rum

Into a shot glass, layer each ingredient in order with a spoon.

Drink Two Beers Faster than One Shot
Set up two draft beers in pint glasses and a shot of your choice. Challenge a friend that you can drink two beers before he or she can drink one shot. The rules are that you get a one-beer head start, you can't touch each other's glasses, and he or she can't drink until your glass is set down on the table. The trick is that you drink your first beer and turn your glass over the shot. Then drink your second beer.

Cigar Band

½ ounce amaretto
½ ounce Irish cream

½ ounce cognac

Into a shot glass, layer each ingredient in order with a spoon.

Coral Snake Bite

⅓ ounce coffee liqueur
⅓ ounce Galliano
⅓ ounce cherry brandy

Into a shot glass, layer each ingredient in order with a spoon.

Easter Egg

¼ ounce raspberry liqueur   ¼ ounce Parfait Amour
¼ ounce crème de banana   ¼ ounce cream

Into a shot glass, layer each ingredient in order with a spoon.

Green-Eyed Irish Blonde

⅓ ounce melon liqueur   ⅓ ounce Irish cream
⅓ ounce crème de banana

Into a shot glass, layer each ingredient in order with a spoon.

Jack Black

¾ ounce black sambuca   ¾ ounce Jack Daniel's

Into a shot glass, layer each ingredient in order with a spoon.

Mexican Flag

⅓ ounce green crème de menthe   ⅓ ounce sloe gin
⅓ ounce peppermint schnapps

Into a shot glass, layer each ingredient in order with a spoon.

Pirate's Treasure

chilled Goldschläger
chilled Captain Morgan spiced rum

Into a shot glass, layer each ingredient in order with a spoon.
The gold at the bottom is the Pirate's Treasure.

Rhinestone Dallas Cowboy

½ ounce Goldschläger
½ ounce blue curaçao

Into a shot glass, layer each ingredient in order with a spoon.

Silk Panty

¾ ounce black sambuca
¾ ounce peach schnapps

Into a shot glass, layer each ingredient in order with a spoon.

Kahlúa and Cream Trick

You need two shot glasses, one filled with Kahlúa and
the other with cream. Ask your challenger to put the
contents of one glass into the other without pouring any
out (or pouring one in their mouth). They are allowed
one tool—their driver's license. The answer? Lay the
license over the shot glass that contains the Kahlúa,
then turn it upside down on top of the cream without spilling. Slowly remove the license and the Kahlúa
and cream will switch glasses. This works because the
Kahlúa is heavier than the cream.

Slippery Dick

¾ ounce banana liqueur   ¾ ounce Irish cream

Into a shot glass, layer each ingredient in order with a spoon.

Slippery Nipple

¾ ounce sambuca   ¾ ounce Irish cream

Into a shot glass, layer each ingredient in order with a spoon.

Tequila Passion Shot
You'll need salt, lime, a shot of tequila, and a willing partner. To prep the shot: Lick a part of your partner's body, sprinkle the salt on the wet spot, and place the lime, meat side out, between your partner's lips or teeth. To take the shot, lick the salt, drink the tequila, and take a bite of the lime.

Wicked Witch's Socks

⅓ ounce coffee liqueur   ⅓ ounce black vodka
⅓ ounce white crème de cacao

Into a shot glass, layer each ingredient in order with a spoon.

Flaming Shots and Shooters

Flamed shots and shooters are set on fire and much precaution should always be taken when playing with fire. Always make sure everything in the area around and above you is nonflammable. Flames should be blown out before the shot ever reaches your mouth. And always light the shot with a match as opposed to a lighter. With a lighter, you risk contaminating your shot with lighter fluid.

Bailey's Comet

1½ ounces Bailey's Irish Cream   several pinches cinnamon
⅛ ounce 151 rum

Pour the Bailey's Irish Cream into a shot glass. Slowly layer the 151 rum on top of the Bailey's, then light with a match. When you see the flame, sprinkle cinnamon on the flame and it will make tiny fireworks-type sparkles, creating a comet effect. After the flame burns out, drink.

Dragon's Breath

½ ounce green crème de menthe   ⅛ ounce Grand Marnier
½ ounce gold tequila

Into a shot glass, carefully layer each ingredient in order with a spoon. Light the Grand Marnier with a match; allow the flame to die out, then drink.

Eternal Flame

½ ounce Dooley's Toffee Liqueur   ¾ ounce Grand Marnier
½ ounce coffee liqueur   Reese's Peanut Butter Cup

Pour the toffee liqueur, coffee liqueur, and ½ ounce of Grand Marnier in a shot glass. Take a spoon and scoop out a little of the middle of the Reese's Peanut Butter Cup. Eat the middle and set the rest of the peanut butter cup on top of the shot glass. Pour in the remaining ¼ ounce of Grand Marnier into the scooped out area and light. When the flame dies, drink the shot and eat the candy.

Hot Apple Pie

¼ ounce sour apple schnapps
¼ ounce cinnamon schnapps
¼ ounce Irish cream
¼ ounce Captain Morgan spiced rum
⅛ ounce 151 rum
squirt of whipped cream

Pour the apple schnapps, cinnamon schnapps, Irish cream, and Captain Morgan rum in a shot glass. Carefully float the 151 rum on top and light. Put out the flame by squirting whipped cream on top. Eat the whipped cream and drink the shot.

Jell-O Shot Hints

You'll have to make some space in your fridge to set the Jell-O shots. The cheapest method is to measure the space in your fridge and cut out cardboard or foam board squares to create a stacking system: cardboard, layer of shots, cardboard, layer of shots, cardboard, layer of shots, and so on. As to what kind of Jell-O shots to make, well, it's limited only by your imagination. Most people start with a real drink and then look for the flavors of Jell-O and spirits to make them into miniature bite-size versions.

Hot Blooded

1½ ounces tequila
several dashes Tabasco
⅛ ounce 151 rum

Pour the tequila into a shot glass and add several dashes of Tabasco. Gently layer the 151 rum on top, then light. Allow the flame to die out, then drink.

S'mores

½ ounce dark crème de cacao
¼ ounce butterscotch schnapps
¼ ounce Irish cream
⅛ ounce 151 rum
toothpick stuck with 2 miniature marshmallows

Pour the first three ingredients in a shot glass. Float the 151 rum on top. Light the rum, roast the marshmallows, then drink the shot after the fire has died down.

Statue of Liberty

⅓ ounce grenadine
⅓ ounce white crème de cacao
⅓ ounce blue curaçao
⅛ ounce 151 rum

Into a shot glass, carefully layer each ingredient in order with a spoon. Light, hold up like the Statue of Liberty, blow out the flame, and drink. It will taste like a chocolate-covered cherry.

Wish upon a Burning Star

star fruit slice
1 teaspoon raw sugar
pinch cinnamon
1½ ounces Goldschläger
⅛ ounce 151 rum
bamboo skewer

Dip the star fruit into the raw sugar and cinnamon. Into a shot glass, pour the Goldschläger and half of the rum on top. Skewer the star fruit, pour on the remaining rum, and hold over the flame to light. Make a wish, blow out the flames, drink the shot, then eat the star fruit.

Drops and Bombs

The original name for drops and bombs is a Boilermaker (shot of whiskey dropped into a beer). The words "drops" and "bombs" gained popularity about a decade ago.

Boilermaker

1½ ounces whiskey
half glass beer

Pour a shot of whiskey into the shot glass and fill a glass half-way with beer. Drop the shot into the beer and chug.

Burning Busch

1 bottle Busch beer
1 ounce Southern Comfort
⅛ ounce 151 rum

Pour a bottle of Busch beer into a beer glass. In a shot glass, pour in the Southern Comfort and carefully layer the 151 rum on top. Light the shot and let it burn for a bit to burn most of the rum away. Drop into the beer and chug.

Flaming Dr. Pepper

⅛ ounce grenadine
1 ounce amaretto
¼ ounce 151 rum
half glass light beer

Pour the first three ingredients into a shot glass and half-fill a glass with beer. Light the shot and drop the shot glass into the beer. Chug.

Irish Car Bomb

½ ounce Irish whiskey
½ ounce Irish cream

8 ounces Guinness Stout

Pour Irish whiskey and Irish cream into a shot glass. Drop it into a glass of Guinness. Chug before the drink curdles.

Jäger Bomb

Red Bull

1 ounce Jägermeister

Pour a can of Red Bull into a glass and drop a shot of Jägermeister in. Drink.

Red Bull
Red Bull may seem like a new product, but it has been around since the early 1960s in Asia. It was very popular among blue-collar workers. By the early 1990s it reached Europe, and then the United States in the late 1990s. Now you see it everywhere.

Lunch Box

3½ ounces orange juice
1½ ounces beer

1½ ounces amaretto
1½ ounces Southern Comfort

Pour the orange juice and beer into a highball glass. Then take a shot glass and pour in the amaretto and Southern Comfort. Drop the shot glass into the highball glass, then chug.

Sake to Me

1¼ ounces sake
¼ ounce 151 rum

half glass beer
chopsticks

Pour the shot of sake and float the rum on top. Pour beer into a glass until it is half full. Lay the chopsticks on top of the glass, and balance the shot glass on top of the chopsticks. Light the shot and karate-chop the bar top—the shot will drop into the beer. Chug.

Chapter 12

Multi-Spirited Specialty Drinks

When a Long Island Iced Tea recipe calls for vodka, gin, rum, tequila, and triple sec, which chapter should it be in? You see the dilemma. These recipes are multi-spirited. Some are frozen, while others are on the rocks or served chilled straight up. You'll find classic, tropical, hot, juicy, creamy, and sour recipes all living together here.

Multi-Spirited Drink History

Popular lore tells us that one of the first cocktails was a multi-spirited drink, mixed in New Orleans in the early 1800s. The Sazerac was made with rye whiskey, absinthe, bitters, and sugar. There have been many punches and sangrias since then, but it's believed that the multi-spirited froufrou seed was planted when T.G.I. Friday's opened the first casual bar and grill in New York City in 1965. Friday's was first to create a cocktail menu to go alongside the food menu, a tradition it proudly carries on today.

By the late 1970s, hundreds of imitative bar and grills opened nationwide, and all had menus advertising multi-spirited drinks full of the flavors of the time: coffee liqueur; Irish cream; amaretto; blue curaçao; crème de cacao, menthe, noyaux, and banana; flavored brandies; grenadine; and Midori. Between the 1980s and 2000s the menus exploded, thanks to a glut of new products flooding the market, including schnapps in all flavors, crème liqueurs in all flavors, and every category of spirit infused with every flavor imaginable. The results of these new tastes can be found in the drinks in this chapter.

Multi-Spirited Recipes

57 Chevy

½ ounce vodka
1½ ounces Southern Comfort
½ ounce Grand Marnier
½ ounce amaretto
orange juice to fill

Pour the first four ingredients into a tall glass of ice. Fill with orange juice.

57 Chevy with Hawaiian License Plates

½ ounce vodka
1½ ounces Southern Comfort
½ ounce Grand Marnier

½ ounce amaretto
pineapple juice to fill

Pour the first four ingredients into a tall glass of ice. Fill with pineapple juice.

Acapulco Zombie

1 ounce tequila
1 ounce vodka
1 ounce rum

¼ ounce apricot brandy
orange and grapefruit juice to fill

Pour the first four ingredients into a tall glass of ice. Fill with orange and grapefruit juice.

Ace Ventura

1 ounce vodka
¼ ounce tequila
¼ ounce rum
¼ ounce sambuca red
¼ ounce sambuca blue

¼ ounce sambuca green
¼ ounce sambuca black
¼ ounce sambuca white
¼ ounce sambuca gold
Sprite or 7-Up to fill

Pour the vodka, tequila, rum, and sambucas into a tall glass of ice. Fill with Sprite or 7-Up.

Adam and Eve

1 ounce Forbidden Fruit liqueur
½ ounce gin

½ ounce apple brandy
¼ ounce lemon juice

Shake all ingredients with ice. Strain into a martini glass.

AK-47

¼ ounce brandy
¼ ounce whiskey
¼ ounce gin
¼ ounce vodka
¼ ounce rum

¼ ounce bourbon
¼ ounce Cointreau
1 ounce lime juice
club soda to fill

Pour the liquors and lime juice into a tall glass of ice. Fill with club soda.

Alabama Slammer

½ ounce vodka
½ ounce Southern Comfort
½ ounce amaretto

½ ounce sloe gin
orange juice to fill

Pour the first four ingredients into a tall glass of ice. Fill with orange juice.

Aloha

¼ ounce dark rum
¼ ounce dry vermouth
¼ ounce cognac

¼ ounce gin
1 ounce fresh lime juice

Shake all ingredients with ice. Strain into a martini glass.

Alpine Lemonade

1 ounce vodka
1 ounce gin

1 ounce rum
lemonade and cranberry
juice to fill

Pour the vodka, gin, and rum into a tall glass of ice. Fill with equal parts of lemonade and cranberry juice.

Alternatini

3 ounces vodka
¼ ounce white crème de cacao

¼ ounce sweet vermouth
¼ ounce dry vermouth

Shake all ingredients with ice. Strain into a martini glass.

Angel's Fall

1 ounce amaretto
½ ounce gin
½ ounce vodka
½ ounce 151 rum
½ ounce dark rum
1 ounce grenadine
cranberry, pineapple, and grapefruit juice to fill

Pour the liquors and grenadine into a tall glass of ice. Fill with equal parts cranberry, pineapple, and grapefruit juice.

Apple Pie

1 ounce rum
½ ounce sweet vermouth
1 teaspoon apple brandy

1 ounce lemon juice
½ teaspoon grenadine

Combine all ingredients in a shaker half filled with ice. Shake well. Strain into a cocktail glass.

Around the World

½ ounce Russian vodka
½ ounce Caribbean rum
½ ounce Italian amaretto

½ ounce tequila
½ ounce Jägermeister
Hawaiian Punch to fill

Pour the first five ingredients into a tall glass of ice. Fill with Hawaiian Punch.

Barbary Coast

½ ounce Scotch
½ ounce gin
½ ounce rum

½ ounce white crème de cacao
½ ounce cream

Shake all ingredients with ice. Strain into a martini glass.

Big Banana!

1 ounce banana rum
1 ounce amaretto
1 ounce coconut rum

1 ounce crème de banana
pineapple juice to fill

Pour the first four ingredients into a tall glass of ice. Fill with pineapple juice.

Bionic Tonic

1 ounce Chambord
1 ounce Alizé Gold Passion
1 ounce vodka
club soda to fill

Pour each ingredient one by one over a short glass of ice. They will layer on top of one another.

Cocktails in the Sky
The first in-flight cocktails were served to paying passengers on the Zeppelin (airship) flying over Germany. The year was 1910.

🍸 Black Maria

2 ounces light rum
1 ounce coffee-flavored
  brandy

3 ounces cold strong black coffee
2 teaspoons fine sugar

Pour all ingredients into a brandy snifter and stir. Add ice.

Blue Knickers

1 ounce vodka
1 ounce blue curaçao
1 ounce Galliano

1 ounce pineapple juice
1¼ ounces cream

Shake the first four ingredients with ice. Strain into a martini glass. Slowly float the cream on top.

Blue Velvetini

sugar for rimming
blue food coloring
1 ounce light rum

1 ounce blue curaçao
1 ounce blueberry schnapps
2 ounces white (clear)
  cranberry juice

Mix the sugar and a few drops of blue food coloring on a saucer with a spoon. Wet the rim of a martini glass with water and dip the rim into the blue sugar. Shake the rum, curaçao, blueberry schnapps, and white cranberry juice with ice. Strain into the glass.

☑ Bolero

1½ ounces light rum
¾ ounce calvados or apple brandy
1 teaspoon sweet vermouth

Combine ingredients in a mixing glass half filled with ice. Stir well. Pour into an old-fashioned glass with ice.

☑ Boston Sidecar

1 ounce light rum
½ ounce brandy
¾ ounce Triple Sec
1 ounce lime juice or juice of half a lime

Combine ingredients in a shaker nearly filled with ice. Strain into a cocktail glass.

Brass Monkey

1 ounce vodka
1 ounce rum
fresh orange juice to fill

Pour vodka and rum into a highball glass of ice. Fill with orange juice.

Cherry Blossom

5 pitted sour cherries
½ ounce lemon juice
½ ounce Cherry Heering liqueur
½ ounce curaçao
1½ ounces brandy

Muddle cherries with lemon juice and liqueurs in a mixing glass. Add brandy and ice. Shake, then strain into a cocktail glass.

Continental

1½ ounces light rum
½ ounce green crème de menthe
½ teaspoon fine sugar

1 tablespoon lime juice
1 teaspoon lemon juice
lemon twist

Combine ingredients in a shaker nearly filled with ice. Strain into a cocktail glass. Serve with a lemon twist.

Corkscrew

1½ ounces light rum
½ ounce peach-flavored brandy

½ ounce dry vermouth
lemon twist

Combine ingredients in a shaker nearly filled with ice. Strain into a cocktail glass. Serve with a lemon twist.

Corpse Reviver

1 ounce gin
½ ounce Cointreau
½ ounce Lillet Blanc

¾ ounce fresh lemon juice
¼ ounce absinthe substitute

Shake all ingredients with ice. Strain into a martini glass.

A Guy Walks into a Bar

A guy walks into a bar and asks for ten shots of the finest gin. The bartender sets him up, and the guy takes the first shot in the row and pours it on the floor. He then takes the last shot and does the same. The bartender asks, "Why did you do that?" And the guy replies, "Well the first shot always tastes like crap, and the last one always makes me sick!"

Dixie Whiskey

1½ ounces bourbon whiskey
½ ounce orange curaçao
¼ ounce white crème de menthe

2¼ ounces angostura bitters
¾ ounce fresh lemon juice

Shake all ingredients with ice. Strain into a martini glass.

Dutchie

1 ounce cherry brandy
1 ounce crème de banana
1 ounce apricot brandy

milk
1 ounce advocaat, chilled

Pour the first three ingredients into a tall glass of ice. Fill three-quarters full with milk. Slowly pour the advocaat over the top of the milk and watch as the advocaat drips around the ice and through the milk.

El Chico

1½ ounces light rum
½ ounce sweet vermouth
¼ teaspoon grenadine

¼ teaspoon curaçao
cherry and lemon twist

Combine liquid ingredients in a shaker nearly filled with ice. Strain into a cocktail glass. Serve with cherry and lemon twist.

A Guy Walks into a Bar

A guy walks into a bar, sits down, and hears a small voice say, "You look nice today." A few minutes later, he again hears a small voice: "That's a nice shirt." The guy asks the bartender, "Who is that?" The bartender says, "Those are the peanuts. They're complimentary!"

Electric Iced Tea

½ ounce vodka
½ ounce gin
½ ounce rum
½ ounce tequila

½ ounce blue curaçao
1 ounce sour mix
splash Sprite or 7-Up

Pour all ingredients into a tall glass of ice. Stir.

El Presidente

1½ ounces light rum
¾ ounce curaçao

¾ ounce dry vermouth
¼ ounce grenadine

Shake all ingredients with ice. Strain into a martini glass.

Embassy Cocktail

¾ ounce brandy
¾ ounce Cointreau
¾ ounce Appleton Jamaican rum

½ ounce fresh lime juice
¼ ounce angostura bitters

Shake all ingredients with ice. Strain into a martini glass.

Feliz Natal

1 ounce port
1 ounce amaretto

2 ounces crème de cacao
1 ounce cherry brandy

Stir all ingredients together in a short glass of ice. Stir.

Floridita

1½ ounces rum
½ ounce sweet vermouth
⅛ ounce white crème de cacao

½ ounce lime juice
⅛ ounce grenadine

Shake all ingredients with ice. Strain into a martini glass.

Fog Cutter

2 ounces white rum
1 ounce brandy
½ ounce gin
2 ounces fresh lemon juice

1 ounce fresh orange juice
½ ounce orgeat syrup
½ ounce sweet sherry

Shake everything but the sherry with ice. Strain into a tall glass of ice. Float the sherry on top.

Foggy Afternoon

1 ounce vodka
½ ounce apricot brandy
½ ounce triple sec

1¼ ounces crème de banana
1¼ ounces fresh lemon juice

Shake all ingredients with ice. Strain into a martini glass.

Golden Friendship

1 ounce light rum
1 ounce sweet vermouth
1 ounce amaretto
4 ounces ginger ale
cherry

Pour rum, vermouth, and amaretto into a Collins glass with ice. Add ginger ale. Garnish with a cherry.

Hand Grenade

1 ounce 151 rum
1 ounce vodka
1 ounce melon liqueur
1 ounce amaretto
pineapple juice to fill

Pour the first four ingredients into a tall glass of ice. Fill with pineapple juice.

Hawaiian Iced Tea

½ ounce vodka
½ ounce gin
½ ounce light rum
½ ounce tequila

½ ounce triple sec
1 ounce sour mix
1 ounce pineapple juice

Pour all ingredients into a tall glass of ice. Stir.

Honeymoon Cocktail

2 ounces applejack
½ ounce Bénédictine
½ ounce curaçao

½ ounce fresh lemon juice
lemon twist

Shake all liquid ingredients with ice. Strain into a martini glass.
Garnish with a lemon twist.

The Honey Month
In ancient Babylon, for a month after a wedding, the
bride's father supplied his new son-in-law with all the
mead he could drink. Because the Babylonian calendar
was lunar-based, what they called the honey month is
what we know today as the *honeymoon*.

Ice Palace

1 ounce light rum
½ ounce Galliano
½ ounce apricot brandy

2 ounces pineapple juice
¼ ounce fresh lemon juice

Pour all ingredients into a tall glass of ice. Stir.

Irish Shannigan

1½ ounces Irish whiskey
½ ounce light rum
½ ounce sloe gin
1 teaspoon powdered sugar

1 ounce fresh lemon juice
¼ cup fresh peaches
¼ cup fresh raspberries

Combine all ingredients in a blender with ice. Blend, then pour into a tall glass.

K.G.B.

½ ounce kirschwasser
1½ ounces gin
¼ ounce apricot brandy

½ ounce fresh lemon juice
½ teaspoon sugar
lemon twist

Shake liquids and sugar with ice. Strain into a martini glass and garnish with a lemon twist.

Las Vegas, Baby!

½ ounce Seagram's 7
½ ounce Licor 43
½ ounce Pimm's No. 1

½ ounce 151 rum
Sprite or 7-Up to fill

Pour the liquors into a tall glass of ice. Fill with Sprite or 7-Up.

Long Beach Tea

½ ounce vodka
½ ounce gin
½ ounce light rum
½ ounce tequila

½ ounce triple sec
1 ounce sour mix
1 ounce cranberry juice

Pour all ingredients into a tall glass of ice. Stir.

Long Island Iced Tea

½ ounce vodka
½ ounce light rum
½ ounce tequila
½ ounce triple sec

½ ounce gin
1 ounce sour mix
splash of cola

Pour all ingredients into a tall glass of ice. Stir.

Magnum

1 ounce Goldschläger
1 ounce Jack Daniel's
1 ounce rum

1 ounce vodka
2 ounces fruit punch

Blend all ingredients with ice. Pour into a tall glass.

Man Hunting

1½ ounces Wild Turkey 101
1 ounce curaçao

½ ounce sweet vermouth
½ ounce fresh lemon juice

Shake all ingredients with ice. Strain into a martini glass.

Miami Iced Tea

½ ounce vodka
½ ounce gin
½ ounce light rum
½ ounce peach schnapps

½ ounce triple sec
1 ounce sour mix
1 ounce cranberry juice
splash Sprite or 7-Up

Pour all ingredients into a tall glass of ice. Stir.

Miami Vice

The Miami Iced Tea is not the same as a Miami Vice. A Miami Vice is half strawberry daiquiri and half piña colada.

Mojo

1 ounce light rum
1 ounce cherry brandy
3 ounces amber beer
pineapple juice and Sprite to fill

Pour the first three ingredients into a tall glass of ice. Fill with equal parts of pineapple juice and Sprite.

Moonlight Drive

1 ounce vodka
1 ounce rum
1 ounce sloe gin
1 ounce coconut rum
½ ounce amaretto
orange and pineapple juice to fill

Pour the liquors into a tall glass of ice. Fill with juices.

Y Mudslide Martini

1 ounce vodka
1 ounce Irish cream

1 ounce coffee liqueur
1 ounce cream

Shake all ingredients with ice, then strain into a martini glass.

Naked Twister

1 ounce melon liqueur
½ ounce vodka

½ ounce Tuaca
pineapple juice to fill

Pour the first three ingredients into a tall glass of ice. Fill with pineapple juice.

Neapolitan Martini

1 ounce vanilla vodka
1 ounce orange vodka
½ ounce Grand Marnier

½ ounce Parfait d'Amour
splash fresh lime juice
orange twist

Shake all liquid ingredients with ice. Strain into a martini glass. Garnish with an orange twist.

Neapolitan History

Layering three colors or three flavors began in Naples, Italy. These days, the most common name for this layering in Italy is *spumoni*. The most common place to find this layering in America is in your local grocer's freezer. It's called Neapolitan ice cream.

PB&J

1 ounce Frangelico
1 ounce raspberry liqueur
1 ounce raspberry vodka
1 ounce cream

Shake all ingredients with ice. Strain into a martini glass.

PB&J with Bananas

1 ounce Frangelico
½ ounce raspberry liqueur
1 ounce raspberry vodka
1 ounce banana liqueur
1 ounce cream

Shake all ingredients with ice. Strain into a martini glass.

Raspberry Long Island Ice Tea

½ ounce raspberry vodka
½ ounce gin
½ ounce raspberry rum
½ ounce tequila
½ ounce triple sec
1 ounce sour mix
splash Sprite or 7-Up

Pour all ingredients into a tall glass of ice. Stir.

Red Death

¾ ounce vodka
¾ ounce Southern Comfort
¼ ounce sloe gin
¼ ounce triple sec
¼ ounce Rose's lime juice
¼ ounce grenadine
orange juice to fill

Pour liquors and grenadine into a tall glass of ice. Fill with orange juice.

Satan's Whiskers

¾ ounce gin
¾ ounce dry vermouth
¾ ounce sweet vermouth

½ ounce Grand Marnier
½ ounce orange juice
2 dashes orange bitters

Shake all ingredients with ice. Strain into a martini glass.

Sex on the Farm

1 ounce Wild Turkey honey liqueur
½ ounce peach schnapps
½ ounce raspberry liqueur

1 ounce cranberry juice
1 ounce pineapple juice

Shake all ingredients with ice. Strain into a martini glass.

Shalom

1½ ounces gin
½ ounce cherry brandy

½ ounce Madeira
1 ounce orange juice

Shake all ingredients with ice. Strain into a martini glass.

Sloe Comfortable Fuzzy Screw Against the Wall

½ ounce sloe gin
½ ounce Southern Comfort
½ ounce peach schnapps

½ ounce vodka
½ ounce Galliano
orange juice to fill

Pour all ingredients into a highball glass filled with ice. Stir.

Sloe Comfortable Screw

1 ounce sloe gin
1 ounce Southern Comfort

1 ounce vodka
orange juice to fill

Pour all ingredients into a highball glass filled with ice. Stir.

♼ Sloe Comfortable Screw Against the Wall

1 ounce sloe gin
1 ounce Southern Comfort
1 ounce vodka

orange juice to fill
½ ounce Galliano

Pour the first three ingredients into a highball glass filled with ice and stir. Fill with orange juice. Float Galliano on top.

Sloe Comfortable Screw Against the Wall in Mexico

½ ounce sloe gin
½ ounce Southern Comfort
½ ounce vodka

½ ounce tequila
orange juice to fill

Pour all ingredients into a highball glass filled with ice. Stir.

Sloe Comfortable Screw Between the Sheets

½ ounce sloe gin
½ ounce Southern Comfort
½ ounce vodka

½ ounce rum
½ ounce brandy
orange juice to fill

Pour all ingredients into a highball glass filled with ice. Stir.

Cherry Bombs

Buy a gallon of maraschino cherries at a wholesale store. Pour out half of the juice and save for another use. Pour in a bottle of booze (your choice) and let sit in the fridge for at least 24 hours. Great choices of booze are cherry vodka, raspberry rum, or vanilla rum, or use anything else you want. When you are ready to present, pour out the liquid and save for another use, and display the cherries in a big bowl, stems up.

Tango

½ ounce rum
½ ounce sweet vermouth
½ ounce dry vermouth
½ ounce Bénédictine
1 ounce orange juice

Shake all ingredients with ice. Strain into a martini glass.

Texas Ex's

½ ounce sherry
½ ounce brandy
½ ounce Tequila Rose
½ ounce strawberry vodka
1 ounce lemon juice
cranberry juice to fill

Pour all ingredients into a tall glass filled with ice. Stir.

Texas Tea

½ ounce tequila
½ ounce vodka
½ ounce rum
½ ounce triple sec
1 ounce sour mix
splash of cola

Pour all ingredients into a tall glass of ice. Stir.

Three Señoritas Margarita

½ ounce blanco tequila
juice from half a lime
5 ounces sweet-and-sour mix
¾ ounce brandy
¾ ounce Tequila Rose
¾ ounce sherry
3 plastic test tubes

Blend the tequila, lime juice, and sweet-and-sour mix with a cup of ice, then pour into a margarita glass. Fill the first test tube with brandy, the next with Tequila Rose, and the third with sherry. Stick the test tubes in the margarita.

Tropical Rain Forest

½ ounce lemon vodka
½ ounce cherry rum
½ ounce white tequila
½ ounce blue curaçao
½ ounce melon liqueur
cranberry, pineapple, and orange juice to fill
paper parasol and fruit of your choice

Pour the liquors into a tall glass of ice. Fill with equal amounts of cranberry, pineapple, and orange juice. Garnish with paper parasol and fruit of your choice.

Twentieth Century

1½ ounces gin   ½ ounce Lillet Blanc
½ ounce white crème de cacao   ¼ ounce fresh lemon juice

Shake all ingredients with ice. Strain into a martini glass.

Vesper

3 ounces gin   ½ ounce Lillet Blanc
1 ounce vodka   lemon twist

Shake all ingredients with ice. Strain into a martini glass. Garnish with a lemon twist.

Waldorf

1½ ounces bourbon   ½ ounce sweet vermouth
¾ ounce Pernod

Pour all ingredients into a shaker with ice. Shake very well and strain into a martini glass over ice.

Chapter 13

Punches and Party, Holiday, and Seasonal Drinks

Punches and party, holiday, and seasonal drinks stir up a sense of social warmth and togetherness. Most are made in mass quantities and shared with dear friends, family, co-workers, and new acquaintances. They are celebratory by nature.

Punches and Party Drinks

The most important points to know about making and serving mass quantities of punch are these: you should start with everything cold, and you should invite guests to serve themselves by providing everything they need on a well-decorated table. Try to think outside the box. Visit discount stores in the summer to gather fun and inexpensive partyware. To keep punches cold, you can freeze molds made of the punch with some water to float in the punch, make punch bowls out of ice, or rent a cooling champagne fountain from a local party store. If drinks need to be shaken, then hire a local bartender, whip up a batch of what you want in mass quantities, and just have her shake and serve the drinks. Just make sure you set up your drink station at the opposite end—across the room—from the food station for crowd flow. Also, know that any single drink recipe in this chapter can be mass-produced.

Ace of Spades (Casino Party Martini)

Serves 1

2 ounces Blavod black vodka
2 ounces white (clear) crème de cacao

Shake the ingredients with ice, then strain into a martini glass.

Baby Shower Champagne

Serves 1

½ ounce pomegranate juice
nonalcoholic sparkling apple cider or ginger ale
strawberry

Pour the pomegranate juice in a champagne flute. Add the sparkling apple cider or ginger ale. Garnish with a strawberry on the rim.

Bachelorette Strip and Go Naked Punch

Serves 12

1 bottle lime-flavored gin
3 ounces grenadine
12-pack light beer
2 (12-ounce) cans frozen limeade
lime wheels and cherries

Put the gin in the freezer and the grenadine and beer in the fridge; allow the limeade to thaw, then refrigerate. When ready, pour everything (add the beer slowly) into a punch bowl and add the garnishes. Ladle into tall glasses of ice and garnish with lime wheels and cherries. Search the Internet for naughty bachelorette drink items to accompany this punch.

Flash Paper
Popular with magicians for tricks, flash paper provides a quick burst of light when it touches a flame. It can be purchased at any local magic shop. A small piece of it can create a very big, bright flame. Make sure to move your hands away quickly after it lights to make it seem like a magic trick. Since it does require fire, be careful when using it.

Blinded by the Light Girly Birthday Drink

Serves 1

1½ ounces light rum
Crystal Light pink lemonade to fill
glow stick

⅛ ounce 151 rum
flash paper

This is a drink that someone makes for the birthday person. Pour the light rum into a tall glass of ice and fill with the Crystal Light pink lemonade. Crack a glow stick and drop it in the drink. Top the drink with 151 rum, then light. While the drink is flaming, hold and hide flash paper in your palms and light it with the flame.

Divorce Party Blues

Serves 1

½ ounce blue curaçao
¾ glass Sprite or 7-Up

2 ounces Blavod black vodka

Celebrate the mourning (black vodka) of a divorce by getting the blues (blue curaçao)! Pack a tall glass with ice and pour in the blue curaçao. Fill three-quarters of the glass with Sprite or 7-Up, then carefully float the black vodka on top.

Garden Party Sangria (white sangria with rose petals)

Serves 8

2 cups water
1 cup sugar
12 cinnamon sticks
2 bottles non-dry white wine
2 cups sparkling water

2 cups apple juice
1 cup white (clear) cranberry juice
pitcher of roses and rose petals
lots of cherries
3 apples cut in chunks

Heat the water, sugar, and cinnamon sticks to a simmer. Continue to simmer for 5 minutes, then remove from heat. Let the mixture cool to room temperature. Remove the cinnamon

sticks and mix in all remaining liquid ingredients. Chill overnight in the refrigerator. When ready, present the sangria in a
clear self-serve container and put in rinsed rose petals, apple
chunks, and cherries. Decorate the table with remaining rose
petals and roses and glasses of ice with an apple chunk,
cherry, and rose petal on top.

Hawaiian Luau Jungle Juice

Serves 40

2 bottles (750 ml) dark rum
2 bottles (750 ml) light rum
1 gallon orange juice
1 gallon pineapple juice
1 gallon sweet-and-sour mix
1 bottle grenadine
bag of ice

5-gallon Igloo water cooler
brown mailing paper
black magic marker
jar of maraschino cherries
lots of pineapple slices
box of paper parasols

Pour the dark rum, light rum, orange and pineapple juice,
sweet-and-sour mix, and grenadine in the cooler, then add a
bag of ice and stir. Take the brown paper and make tiki-totem
pole designs on it and wrap it around the cooler. Cut a hole
for the spigot. Set the cherries, pineapple slices, and parasols
out around this self-serve tropical oasis.

Housewarming Sangria

Serves 12

2 tablespoons sugar
2 ounces blackberry brandy
1 cup orange juice
1 cup pineapple juice
½ cup cherry juice
3 bottles of chilled Lambrusco red wine

3 cups maraschino cherries
12 thinly sliced orange wheels
12 thinly sliced lemon wheels
12 thinly sliced lime wheels

Combine all ingredients except for the wine and fruits and refrigerate. When ready to serve, pour the chilled wine and chilled mixture together and garnish with the fruit. Prep glasses of ice with fruit as well.

Pineapple Upside-Down Birthday Cake

Serves 1

2 ounces vanilla vodka
1 ounce Irish cream
2 ounces pineapple juice
¼ ounce grenadine

1 cherry
1 canned pineapple ring
1 squirt whipped cream
1 birthday candle

Shake the first three ingredients with ice and strain into a martini glass. Pour in the grenadine (it will sink to the bottom), then drop in the cherry. Float the pineapple ring on top. Squirt whipped cream in the hole of the pineapple ring (this will hold the candle in place). Stick the candle in the whipped cream and light.

Pink Pajama Party Shots

Serves 10

1 bottle chilled Tequila Rose cream liqueur
chocolate shot glasses

Pour chilled Tequila Rose cream liqueur into the chocolate shot glasses and serve on a tray. You can buy chocolate shot glasses on the Internet or make your own. You can find a recipe for them on page 196.

Spa Party Martini

Serves 1

1 ounce organic Rain vodka
½ ounce organic honey liqueur
½ ounce organic ginger liqueur
1 ounce organic fresh lemon juice
½ ounce organic honey
organic cucumber slice

Shake all ingredients with ice and strain into a martini glass. Slip an organic cucumber slice in the glass.

Wedding Cake Martini

Serves 1

1 ounce vanilla vodka
½ ounce amaretto
½ ounce white chocolate liqueur
1 ounce cream

Shake all ingredients with ice and strain into a martini glass.

Wedding Reception Bubbles

Serves 1

½ ounce strawberry vodka
1 ounce strawberry liqueur
dry champagne to fill
strawberry

Pour the strawberry vodka and the strawberry liqueur into a champagne flute and fill with champagne. Garnish the rim with a strawberry.

Holiday and Seasonal Drinks

Humans will find just about any reason, season, or holiday to celebrate. If you plan to throw a big shindig, save money by purchasing liquors and mixers in bulk. However, you'll need to invest in smaller containers to transfer the bulk amount and make serving easier. Using clean gallon jugs helps solve this problem, and when the punch bowl runs out, all you have to do is grab another gallon from the fridge and refill.

> **How Many People Will Be Invited to the Party?**
> It's very important to know the approximate number of people who will be invited, since this is the basis of the math you will do for everything related to the party. How else will you be able to calculate the amounts of food and drink, invitations, napkins, and glasses? Make a list, check it twice, and always invite the naughty *and* the nice for a memorable party.

January–April

These recipes cover seasons and holidays found in January, February, March, and April.

Chinese New Year Champagne

Serves 1

½ ounce lychee liqueur
½ ounce tangerine juice

champagne to fill

Pour the lychee liqueur and tangerine juice into a champagne flute; then add the champagne.

Green Beer (St. Patrick's Day)

Serves 1

1 pint pilsner (yellow beer)
1 drop green food coloring

Pour up a pint of beerthen add one drop green food coloring. This is how all the bars in the world make it.

Kama Sutra (Valentine's Day)

Serves 1

½ ounce Passoã passion fruit liqueur   ginger ale to fill
½ ounce Alizé Red Passion   maraschino cherries
½ ounce DeKuyper Cheri-berri Pucker

Pour the first three ingredients into a tall glass; then add ice. Fill to the top with ginger ale and garnish with maraschino cherries.

Calculating Amounts

Guests at a party will drink about two or three drinks each. One bottle of wine will yield four 6-ounce glasses of wine, and a (750 ml) bottle of liquor will give you around 25 ounces of alcohol. You will also need about half a pound of ice per person.

Kiss from a Rose (Valentine's Day)

Serves 1

1 ounce Shakers Rose Vodka
1 ounce Tequila Rose strawberry cream liqueur
2 ounces cream

Shake all ingredients with ice and strain into a martini glass.

Nutty Irishman-tini (St. Patrick's Day)

Serves 1

1 ounce Irish cream
1 ounce Frangelico
½ ounce Irish whiskey
1 ounce cream

Shake all ingredients with ice and strain into a martini glass.

Ragin' Cajun Mardi Gras Punch

Serves 20

2 (40-ounce) bottles chilled purple grape juice
2 (48-ounce) cans chilled pineapple juice
bunch green seedless grapes
needle and fishing line
1 bottle (750 ml) chilled citrus vodka
1 (2-liter) bottle chilled ginger ale

Make an ice ring: fill half a ring mold with grape juice, freeze, fill with pineapple juice, and freeze again. String the grapes with the needle and fishing line to make beads. Pour the vodka, remaining juices, and ginger ale in a punch bowl. Place the ice ring and the string of grape beads in the bowl.

> **Green, Gold, and Purple**
> This festive punch combines the traditional Mardi Gras colors of green, representing faith; gold, symbolizing power; and purple, denoting justice. It's delicious with or without the alcohol. Try freezing the grape beads.

Sparkling New Year Cheer

Serves 1

1 sugar cube
6 dashes angostura bitters

chilled champagne to fill
lemon twist

Dash a sugar cube with angostura bitters and drop into the bottom of a champagne flute. Fill the flute with champagne. Twist a lemon twist to release the oils, then rub the rim of the glass with the twist and drop it into the drink.

Super Bowl Drop Kick

Serves 1

glass of beer of your choice
1 ounce American whiskey

Fill a beer glass with a beer; then pour American whiskey into a shot glass. Here's where the drop kick comes in: drop the shot into the beer and kick the whole thing (beer and all) down your throat in one fell swoop.

White Chocolate Easter-tini

Serves 1

1 ounce vanilla vodka
1 ounce white chocolate liqueur
2 ounces eggnog

1 ounce cream
jellybeans

Pour the liquids into a shaker tin of ice and shake, then strain into a martini glass. Hide your little Easter eggs by dropping some jellybeans in the glass to sink to the bottom.

May–August

These recipes cover seasons and holidays found in May, June, July, and August.

Blue Skyy Summer

1 ounce Skyy melon vodka
1 ounce blue curaçao
white (clear) cranberry juice and club soda to fill

Pour melon vodka and curaçao into a tall glass of ice. Fill with equal parts white cranberry juice and club soda.

Born on the 4th of July Martini

Serves 1

1½ ounces cherry vodka or rum
3 ounces white cranberry juice

1 maraschino cherry
½ ounce blue curaçao

Pour the cherry vodka or rum and the white (clear) cranberry juice into a shaker tin of ice and shake; then strain into a martini glass. Drop the cherry in to sink to the bottom; then carefully float the blue curaçao on top by pouring it over the back of a spoon.

Canadian Crown (Canada Day)

Serves 1

2 ounces Crown Royal Canadian blended whisky
1 ounce fresh lemon juice
½ ounce simple syrup
½ ounce grenadine
maraschino cherry

Shake all ingredients with ice and strain into a martini glass.
Add the cherry.

Chatham Artillery Punch

Serves 40

1 bottle sweet red wine	1 cup lemon juice
half bottle light rum	4 cups strong tea
half bottle rye whiskey	1 cup orange juice
half bottle gin	1 cup packed brown sugar
half bottle brandy	2 bottles dry champagne

Mix together all ingredients except champagne. Cover and
refrigerate for several days; then stir in the champagne just
before serving. This is the historical summer punch drunk by
U.S. military soldiers at regimental functions.

Champagne Fountain

You can rent one at a local party store and pour in anything you want as long as it doesn't have pulp or seeds.
Setting it up where it can be reached from all sides is
the best. Even though the fountain will have a chiller, it's
best to pour in your chosen mixture when cold.

Cinco De Mayo Martini

Serves 1

1 ounce aged tequila
1 ounce coconut-flavored tequila
½ ounce agave liqueur
2 ounces fresh lime juice
1 ounce simple syrup

Shake all ingredients with ice and strain into a martini glass.

Horse's Neck (Kentucky Derby)

Serves 1

lemon rind spiral (this is historic bar garnish)
dash angostura bitters
ginger ale to fill
2 ounces Kentucky whiskey

To make the horse's neck simply slice into the top of a whole lemon and carefully peel the entire peel off in a spiral. Lower the spiral into a highball glass; then slowly add ice so that the horse's neck is spiraled all the way up the glass. Pour in the whiskey, dash the bitters, and fill with ginger ale.

Mint Julep Punch (Kentucky Derby)

Serves 25

1 cup mint jelly
4 cups distilled water
1 bottle Kentucky bourbon
1 quart (can) pineapple juice
¼ cup fresh lime juice
1 liter lemon and lime soda
mint sprigs

Heat mint jelly in saucepan with 2 cups of the water until the jelly melts, then cool. Add the rest of the ingredients except the soda and stir. Pour into a punch bowl over a block of ice. Add soda and mint and stir gently.

Summertime Slushy

Serves 20

1 bottle (750 ml) vanilla vodka (or any other flavor you want)
1 bottle (750 ml) coconut rum
1 gallon orange juice
1 gallon pineapple juice
2 (2-liter) bottles citrus soda (like Fresca)

Pour the vodka, rum, orange juice, and pineapple juice in a big bowl or pot and stir. Set in the freezer for at least 24 hours or until frozen. When frozen, place two scoops in a tall glass and fill with the citrus soda.

September–December

These recipes cover seasons and holidays found in September, October, November, and December.

Autumn in New York

Serves 1

1 ounce applejack brandy
½ ounce Tuaca

hot apple cider to fill
whipped cream

Pour the applejack brandy and Tuaca in a mug and fill with hot apple cider. Top with whipped cream.

Bloody Punch Bowl Hand

Make a bloody hand to float around in a Halloween punch from cranberry juice and a latex glove. Fill the glove with the juice, tie, freeze, then rip the glove off. Some gloves have talcum powder inside—make sure you rinse it out first.

Devil's Blood (Halloween)

Serves 1

¾ glass cranberry juice
2 ounces Blavod black vodka

Pack a tall glass with ice; then pour the cranberry juice three-quarters to the top. Slowly pour the black vodka on top.

The Grinch's Sour Caramel Apple Pie

Serves 1

raw sugar and crushed graham crackers for rimming
1 ounce cream
1 ounce green apple vodka or rum
1 ounce sour apple schnapps
1 ounce butterscotch schnapps
cinnamon for sprinkling

In a saucer, mix raw sugar and graham crackers; wet the rim of a martini glass with cream and dip it into the sugared crumbs. Shake the rest of the ingredients with ice and strain into a martini glass. Sprinkle with cinnamon.

Holly Berry

Serves 1

1½ ounces raspberry vodka
½ ounce triple sec
¼ ounce Rose's lime juice
3 ounces cranberry juice
washed holly sprig without
  berries (optional)

Pour the raspberry vodka, triple sec, Rose's lime juice, and cranberry juice in a shaker tin of ice, shake, then strain into a martini glass. Garnish with a washed holly sprig without the berries for a festive touch. (Don't eat the berries—they are toxic. Use a plastic replica if you wish.)

Pumpkin Pie

Serves 1

raw sugar and nutmeg for rimming
2 ounces vanilla vodka

1 ounce cream
1 ounce pumpkin schnapps

In a saucer, mix a little raw sugar (the brown kind) and nutmeg; then wet the rim of a martini glass with cream and dip the glass into the sugar and spice. Shake the rest of the ingredients with ice and strain into a martini glass.

Thanksgiving Turkey Cosmo

Serves 1

1½ ounces Wild Turkey bourbon
½ ounce triple sec

¼ ounce lime juice
2 ounces cranberry juice

Shake all ingredients with ice and strain into a martini glass.

Wassail (historic holiday punch)

Serves 12

1 cup filtered water
¼ teaspoon nutmeg
¼ teaspoon cardamom
¼ teaspoon powdered ginger
2 cloves
2 cinnamon sticks

2 bottles medium dry sherry
1 cup raw sugar
3 organic egg yolks
6 organic egg whites
½ cup brandy
4 baked apples

Put the water and spices in a saucepan and simmer for 10 minutes. Add the sherry and sugar; heat, but do not boil. Remove from heat. Lightly beat egg yolks and whites separately (they should just be frothy). Pour a cup of the spiced sherry mix into a punch bowl and stir in the egg yolks, then add the brandy. Beat in the egg whites with a whisk until foamy. Float apples.

Ice Punch Bowl

To make a bowl out of ice you need a very large plastic bowl, a medium-size plastic bowl, a reach-in freezer, some weights, and water. Place the large bowl in the bottom of the freezer and fill halfway with water, then place the medium-size bowl in the water and the weights in the medium bowl. The goal is to weight it down enough to get the water level to rise to the top of the large bowl. You can also use freezer tape. Let it freeze for at least two days. Take it out when you need it and let it thaw naturally until the bowls pop off. (Running water on it weakens it.) Set the ice bowl on top of a platter that has a couple of folded towels under linen to absorb the melting ice. It really doesn't melt as fast as you'd think. Decorate all around the bowl.

You Don't Know Jack-O-Lantern Punch

Serves 15

whole pumpkin
round glass bowl (like a goldfish bowl)
half bottle (750 ml) chilled Jack Daniel's
quarter bottle (750 ml) chilled triple sec
equal parts chilled lemonade and Sprite to fill
glow sticks

Hollow out a large pumpkin and carve out a face. Insert a round clear bowl inside and place in the freezer overnight. When ready to serve, pour the Jack Daniel's, triple sec, lemonade, and Sprite into the bowl and stir. Add the glow sticks and place in a dark area for the best effect.

Chapter 14

Starting from Scratch: Homemade Recipes

Running a lemonade stand probably taught you the basics of making a homemade mix. All you needed was the right proportions of lemon juice, sugar, and water—and voilà! Making your own mixes, liqueurs, and faux spirits is fun and can let you create wonderful personalized gifts as well. Why not create a theme basket around your choice? This is truly a gift that can't be bought.

Homemade Supplies

You'll discover that you'll need a few things you don't normally have in the drawers and cabinets in your kitchen. The recipes included in this chapter may ask for filters. Sieves, mesh, cheesecloth, paper towels, and coffee filters will all work. You will also need wide-mouthed jars with tight, secure lids (like canning jars), bottles (plain or decorative), gallon containers, saucepans, measuring spoons and cups, plastic bags, a funnel, and corks.

The Law

In case you were wondering, you are not allowed to distill your own alcohol without a license. None of the recipes in this book teach you to distill alcohol, and you are allowed to make as much homemade wine, liqueur, or beer as you wish. You just cannot sell it. But you can share it, so go ahead and get started!

Oxygen might be crucial for you to live, but it will kill your creations. It's very important that all containers have tight, secure lids. Once your creations are made, continue to keep the air out by making sure you have a tight seal on your bottle. Lots of people like to use corks. You can buy them at hobby stores and sites online. Also, make sure everything is scrubbed, sanitized, and squeaky clean before starting—especially your hands!

Homemade Recipes

Amaretto

Makes 1 (750-milliliter) bottle

2 cups sugar
1 cup brown sugar
2 cups water
3 cups vodka
¼ cup almond extract
4 teaspoons vanilla extract

Heat sugars and water until boiling and sugars are dissolved. Remove from heat and allow to cool. Add vodka, almond extract, and vanilla extract. Pour into a bottle and seal.

Balloon Wine

Makes 5 bottles

1 large can frozen grape juice, thawed
1 large can frozen apple juice, thawed
¼ teaspoon dry yeast
4 cups sugar
1 gallon distilled water
1 thick toy punching balloon

Mix the juices, yeast, and sugar. Funnel into a glass gallon jug. Fill with distilled water. Attach the balloon to the mouth of the jug, securing it with string. Set the jug in a dark place for three weeks while the balloon inflates. When the balloon deflates, slowly pour the liquid into bottles without disturbing the sediment. Cork bottles. Discard sediment. Chill wine in bottles. Take care if you are allergic to latex; many balloons are made with it.

Bar Punch

Makes 1 gallon

3 cups orange juice
3 cups pineapple juice
3 cups sweet-and-sour mix

1 cup grenadine
water to fill

Pour the first four ingredients into a gallon container. Fill the rest of the way with water, leaving enough room at the top for mixing. Mix.

Basic Bitters

Makes 16 ounces

½ pound dried bitter orange peel
pinch cardamom
pinch caraway or anise

pinch coriander seeds
2 cups grain alcohol
boiling water

Mince the orange peel. Mix the chopped peel with the spices and grain alcohol. Pour into a jar and seal. Let the mixture stand in a cool dark place for 15 to 20 days, agitating it every day. Strain into another jar through a coffee filter. Put the strained seeds and peel in a saucepan and crush. Cover the seeds and peel with boiling water and simmer for 5 minutes. Pour into the jar and let stand for 2 days. Strain again and let sit until clear.

Bitters

Best known for their use in flavoring drinks, bitters have also been lauded over the centuries for their ability to aid digestion, stimulate the appetite, and cure hangovers.

Bloody Mary Mix

Makes 16 cups

2 (46-ounce) cans tomato juice
1 teaspoon celery salt
4 ounces lemon juice
1 (5-ounce) bottle Lea & Perrins Worcestershire sauce
Tabasco sauce to taste
salt to taste

Mix all ingredients and refrigerate. You can add many types of ingredients to a basic Bloody Mary mix: raw horseradish, lime juice, A1 steak sauce, a beef bouillon cube, wasabi, chili powder, bitters. You can also try substituting V8 for the regular tomato juice.

Coffee Liqueur

Makes 1 (750-milliliter) bottle

4 cups sugar
1 cup brown sugar
5 cups water
1 cup instant coffee granules
5 tablespoons vanilla extract
half bottle (750 ml) premium vodka

Heat the sugars and the water until mixture boils. Stir until all sugars are dissolved. Remove from heat. Let cool to room temperature. Mix the sugar water, instant coffee, vanilla extract, and vodka together. Bottle the mixture and let it sit undisturbed in a cool dark place for at least a month.

Cranberry Juice

Makes 1 (750-milliliter) bottle

4 cups of fresh cranberries or frozen cranberries, thawed
½–1 cup sugar
water to taste

Process the cranberries in a juicer. Add the sugar (you can also use a cup of Splenda or a cup of apple juice as a sweetener) to make a cranberry concentrate. Add water little by little and taste-test along the way until it reaches the desired tart-and-sweet balance. Refrigerate.

> **The Cranberry**
> Cranberries are one of the three fruits that are native to America. The other two are Concord grapes and blueberries.

Drunken Olives

Makes ½ gallon

½ gallon jar olives	11 ounces gin
11 ounces vodka	11 ounces dry vermouth

Pour out three-quarters of the olive juice (save and refrigerate for Dirty Martinis). Pour in the vodka, gin, and dry vermouth. Put the lid back on and refrigerate. Within 24 hours you will have drunken olives to eat or use in Martinis.

Eggnog

Makes 1 (750-milliliter) bottle

6 organic eggs	1 teaspoon pure vanilla extract
¼ cup sugar	¼ teaspoon fresh ground nutmeg
¼ teaspoon salt	¼ teaspoon fresh ground cinnamon
1 quart milk	

Beat eggs, sugar, and salt in a saucepan. Stir in 2 cups of the milk over low heat. Cook until thick, stirring constantly. The mixture will thinly coat a wooden spoon. Remove from heat and mix in the remaining milk and the vanilla extract. Cover and chill overnight. Stir in the nutmeg and cinnamon.

Faux Absinthe

Makes 1 (750-milliliter) bottle

2 teaspoons dried wormwood
1 fifth premium vodka
4 crushed cardamom pods
2 teaspoons chopped angelica root
2 teaspoons crushed anise seed
½ teaspoon crushed fennel seed
½ teaspoon ground coriander
1 teaspoon marjoram

Place wormwood in vodka for two days. Filter and add remaining spices and herbs. Let sit for one week. Filter and bottle. When serving, drop a sugar cube in the bottom of a cordial glass. The drink will taste faintly like licorice, which comes from the anise.

Wormwood
Wormwood comes from a plant of the same name. It is known for its bitter taste. Find it by searching on the Internet.

Faux Aquavit

Makes 1 (750-milliliter) bottle

1 fifth potato vodka
2 teaspoons caraway seeds
2 teaspoons dill seeds
2 star anise
2 teaspoons cumin seeds
1 teaspoon fennel seeds
1 teaspoon coriander seeds
1 whole clove
1 cinnamon stick

Pour the vodka into a jar and add the rest of the ingredients. Seal tightly and shake. Store in a cool, dark place for 2 to 3 weeks, shaking every 3 or 4 days. Strain and bottle. Place in the freezer.

Faux Drambuie

Makes 1 (750-milliliter) bottle

⅔ (750 ml) bottle premium blended Scotch whisky
1 teaspoon fresh chopped rosemary
1 cup honey

Pour the Scotch into a wide-mouthed jar. Add the rosemary. Cover and let stand for 24 hours, then strain into another jar. Add honey. Shake the mixture. Let age in a dark place for 2 to 3 weeks. Strain through a coffee filter. Pour into a clean bottle.

Faux Galliano

Makes 1 (750-milliliter) bottle

3 cups filtered water
2 cups sugar
1 cup white Karo corn syrup
1 fifth 100 proof premium vodka
6 drops anise extract
3 drops banana extract
1 split vanilla pod
2 or 3 drops yellow food coloring

Boil water and sugar for 5 minutes to make a simple syrup. Remove from heat and let cool. Add Karo syrup, vodka, anise extract, and banana extract. Stir thoroughly, then pour into a wide-mouthed container and drop in the split vanilla pod. Let sit for 24 hours in a dark place. Strain into a sterilized fifth bottle. Add food coloring.

Faux Pimm's No. 1

Makes 1 (750-milliliter) bottle

14 ounces premium gin
7 ounces sweet vermouth
3 ounces sweet sherry or ruby port

1 ounce Cointreau
1 clean 750-ml bottle

Pour all ingredients into a fifth bottle (750 ml). Cap or cork. Turn over once or twice and it's ready to serve.

Another Use for Faux Pimm's No. 1
To make a popular cocktail with your Faux Pimm's No. 1, pour 1½ ounces into a short glass of ice and fill with Sprite or 7-Up. Garnish with a sprig of mint, orange slice, and cucumber slice. Push the garnishes into the drink.

Flavored/Infused Spirits

Makes 1 (750-milliliter) bottle

2 cups fruit, spice, or herb of your choice
1 (750-ml) bottle of vodka, gin, rum, or bourbon

Place your chosen fruit, spice, or herb in the container. Add the alcohol and close the lid tightly. Remove from direct sunlight and let sit from 4 days to 2 weeks. Strain and bottle when finished.

Flexible Ice Pack

1 ice pack

1 cup vodka or any spirit 80 proof or more
1 cup water
1 zippered freezer bag

Pour the vodka and water into the freezer bag and try to get as much of the air out before sealing. Put bag into freezer. The next time you need a slushy ice pack to soothe your face or any other body part, it'll be ready for you.

Ginger Beer

Makes 1 gallon

1½ cups sugar
2 ounces grated gingerroot
lemon zest and juice from 1 lemon
1 gallon boiling water
1 tablespoon yeast

Mix the sugar, grated gingerroot, and lemon zest. Pour the boiling water into the mix and let sit until lukewarm, then strain. Add the lemon juice and the yeast and let mixture stand overnight. Pour into jars or tightly corked bottles the next morning and place in the refrigerator until you need it.

Limoncello

Makes 1 bottle

zest from 7 organic lemons
1 (750-ml) bottle vodka
1 cup simple syrup

Wash the lemons well. Pour half of the vodka in a gallon glass jar and add zest. Cover and let sit at room temperature for 20 days. Add the simple syrup and remaining vodka and let sit for another 20 days. Strain and bottle; then place in the freezer.

Hot Buttered Rum Mix

Makes 25 servings

3 cups brown sugar
½ cup butter
2 tablespoons honey
1 tablespoon rum extract

1 tablespoon vanilla extract
½ teaspoon ground nutmeg
1 teaspoon ground cinnamon
½ teaspoon ground allspice

Combine all ingredients and beat with a mixer until smooth. Put in jar with a tight lid. Store in the refrigerator.

Hot Buttered Rum Ice Cube

You can fill sections of an ice-cube tray halfway with the hot buttered rum mixture. Just pop a cube out when needed. To make a hot buttered rum drink, simply pour 1½ ounces of light or dark rum in a coffee mug, add one frozen cube, and fill with hot water.

Instant Cappuccino Mocha Mix

Makes 25 servings

6 tablespoons plus 2 teaspoons instant espresso coffee powder
3 heaping tablespoons unsweetened cocoa
1¼ cups powdered nondairy creamer
½ cup sugar
2 teaspoons ground cinnamon

Mix all ingredients in a bowl or plastic bag. Store tightly covered until needed. Make a cup by using 4 tablespoons in a cup of hot water.

Irish Cream

Makes 1 (750-milliliter) bottle

¾ cup Irish whiskey
1 (14-ounce) can Eagle Brand condensed milk
1 cup whipping cream
4 eggs
2 tablespoons chocolate-flavored syrup
2 teaspoons instant coffee granules
1 teaspoon vanilla extract

Blend all ingredients until smooth. Store in a tightly covered container in the refrigerator. It can be served within 24 hours and will last for one month. Always stir before serving.

Mead

Makes 4 (750-milliliter) bottles

1 gallon water   ½ tablespoon nutmeg
2½ pounds honey   1 package ale or champagne yeast
juice from 1 lemon

Boil the water and honey. Add the lemon juice and nutmeg. Skim the foam that rises to the surface. Remove from heat and cool to room temperature. Add the yeast. Cover and let sit at room temperature for 15 to 17 days—any longer and the yeast will make the mixture explosive. Bottle in glass containers with tight lids or corks and age for 2 weeks. Refrigerate.

Mint Bourbon

Makes 1 (750-milliliter) bottle

1 bottle premium bourbon   handful of fresh spearmint

Put bourbon and spearmint in a large-mouthed jar. Seal, shake, and set in a cool dark place for 3 weeks. Strain, then bottle.

Peach Purée

Makes 1 cup

5 ripe organic peaches   a little water
squeeze from a lemon wedge

Drop the peaches into boiling water for about 15 seconds. Remove from the pot and set out on paper towels. Pit the peaches, remove skin, and cut into pieces. Put pieces into a food processor with the squeeze of lemon. Add water to reach a desired purée consistency. Refrigerate and stir before using.

Raspberry Liqueur

Makes 2½ cups

1 pint fresh raspberries   ¼ teaspoon whole allspice
2½ cups vodka   ½ cup simple syrup
1 vanilla bean

Wash berries and lightly crush to release flavor. Place berries in a bottle and add vodka, vanilla bean, and allspice. Stir and store in a large-mouthed bottle in cool dark place for 3 weeks. Strain mixture through a cheesecloth and squeeze as much juice as possible. Pour back in bottle and add simple syrup to taste. Age another 3 to 5 weeks.

Sangria #2

8 glasses

2 bottles red wine   3 cups maraschino cherries
2 tablespoons sugar   1 thinly sliced orange wheel
2 ounces brandy   1 thinly sliced lemon wheel
1 cup orange juice   1 thinly sliced lime wheel
½ cup pineapple juice   fruit garnishes
½ cup cherry juice

Combine the liquids and the cherries and half of the sliced fruit. Chill. When ready to serve, add the rest of the fruit. Garnish glasses with a piece of fruit. To make a nonalcoholic version, use grape juice. You are not limited to these fruits. All fruits are acceptable in sangria, so experiment.

Schnapps

Makes 1 (750-milliliter) bottle

⅔ cup granulated sugar
4 cups corn syrup

4 cups vodka
1½ tablespoons peppermint extract

Combine sugar and corn syrup in saucepan over medium heat until sugar dissolves. Remove from heat. Allow mixture to cool. Add the vodka and peppermint extract. Pour in a bottle and seal. To make cinnamon, root beer, or any other flavored schnapps, simply use that flavored extract.

Simple Syrup

Makes 2 cups

2 cups sugar

2 cups water

Pour the sugar and the water in a pan on the stove. Heat until the mixture boils, stirring constantly. Reduce the heat and continue to stir for another 5 minutes. Remove from heat and allow to cool. You can store in the refrigerator for a very long time.

No-Heat Simple Syrup

To make a quick "no-heat" simple syrup, fill a bottle half with sugar and half with water. Shake. After the cloudiness clears, shake again. For sugar-free simple syrup, substitute Splenda for sugar.

Spiced Cider

Makes 1 gallon

1 gallon apple cider
1 teaspoon allspice
½ teaspoon ground cinnamon

½ teaspoon ground cloves
1 cinnamon stick

Pour all ingredients into a pot and simmer for one hour. You can also put everything into a slow cooker and set on warm. Serve warm.

Sweet-and-Sour/Margarita Mix

Makes 6 cups

1 cup fresh lemon juice
1 cup fresh lime juice

3 cups sugar or Splenda
6 cups water

Mix all ingredients together, adjusting the amount of sugar or Splenda according to your personal preference. Making sweet-and-sour mix has personal preference issues. Some people like it sweeter and others more sour. Keep taste-testing until you find your preference.

Other Sweet-and-Sour Mixes

This is an all-purpose sweet-and-sour mix. To make a sour mix for drinks like a Whiskey Sour, Amaretto Sour, or Tom Collins, omit the limes and use all lemons for the recipe. For a margarita you can omit the the lemon juice.

White Sangria #2

Serves 6

1 cup water
½ cup sugar
6 cinnamon sticks
1 bottle non-dry white wine
1 cup sparkling water
1 cup apple juice
½ cup orange juice
3 oranges cut in wheels
cherries to taste
3 apples cut in chunks

Heat the water, sugar, and cinnamon sticks to a simmer. Continue to simmer for 5 minutes. Remove from heat. Let cool to room temperature. Remove the sticks; mix in white wine, sparkling water, apple juice, and orange juice. Chill overnight in the refrigerator. Add the fruit on top for presentation.

No Rules for Sangria

There are no real rules for sangria except that it needs to have wine and fruit in it. For the white sangria, you can easily add or substitute clear liquids like white cranberry juice, white grape juice, champagne (for carbonation), and any seasonal fruits you desire. It's all up to you.

Chapter 15

Mocktails

Mocktails are exactly what they sound like— mock cocktails. They are also called nonalcoholic drinks, alcohol-free drinks, or virgin drinks. In their most basic form, simply omitting the alcohol from a cocktail will create a mocktail. However, you want to be a little more creative than just leaving the vodka out of a Screwdriver.

Reasons for Mocktails

There are countless reasons to select a mocktail—pregnancy, being the designated driver, taking certain medications, dislike of alcohol, being under drinking age, personal choice, or allergies. Mocktails can be frozen, juicy, creamy, sour, sweet, hot, fizzy, spicy, or any other category, just like a regular cocktail.

The most famous mocktail is called a Shirley Temple (today, people also call it a Kiddie Cocktail or a Cherry Sprite). It was named after the famous child actress from the 1930s and believed to be created by a Hollywood bartender from Chasen's Restaurant. The Shirley Temple consisted of ginger ale and grenadine garnished with a maraschino cherry.

Syrups

Torani and Monin syrups are the most popular beverage syrups on the market. They are prevalent in coffee shops. There are about sixty flavors, ranging from Blood Orange to Mojito Mint, and also offer sugar-free alternatives. You'll find that they add a ton of flavor without any alcohol.

The Roy Rogers is probably the second most popular mocktail. It came out in the 1950s and consists of cola and grenadine (Cherry Coke) garnished with a maraschino cherry. Its namesake was a clean-cut, strait-laced singing cowboy with his own TV show in the 1950s.

Today, mocktails can be made with veggies (like cucumbers), herbs, nonalcoholic wine, rum extracts, flavored syrups, and just about anything else you can imagine.

Mocktail Recipes

Anna Banana

1 banana, sliced   ½ ounce coconut cream
5 ounces pineapple juice

Combine ingredients in a blender with ice. Blend thoroughly, then pour into a tall glass.

Baby Bellini

2 ounces peach nectar   chilled sparkling cider to fill

Pour peach nectar into a champagne flute. Fill with sparkling cider.

Big as the MoonPie

4 vanilla wafers   cream for consistency
2 scoops banana ice cream   whipped cream

Crush three of the vanilla wafers and put into a tall glass. Put the banana ice cream in a blender and add cream little by little to reach a smooth consistency. Pour into a glass and garnish with whipped cream and the fourth vanilla wafer.

MoonPie

The Chattanooga Bakery in Tennessee conceived the MoonPie—a graham cracker and marshmallow confection dipped in chocolate—in the early 1900s. It was developed for the local miners who wanted a snack that fit in their lunch pails. They wanted something that was solid and filling.

Blue Hawaiian Shake

½ cup blueberries, fresh or frozen
2 ounces coconut cream
4 ounces milk

Combine ingredients in a blender with ice. Blend thoroughly, then pour into a tall glass.

Blushin' Berry Mary

½ cup fresh raspberries
½ cup strawberry milk
1 cup lemon yogurt
½ cup milk
whipped cream, strawberries, blueberries, and raspberries

Add the fresh raspberries, strawberry milk, lemon yogurt, and milk in a blender. Blend until mixture reaches a smooth consistency. Pour into a tall glass. Garnish with whipped cream, strawberries, blueberries, and raspberries.

Cherry Coke

2 ounces grenadine
cola to fill
maraschino cherry

Pour liquid ingredients over ice in a highball glass. Garnish with a cherry.

Chocolate-Dipped Strawberry

1 tablespoon chocolate or white chocolate syrup
1 ounce light cream
strawberry soda to fill

Pour chocolate and cream into a tall glass. Stir. Fill the glass with ice and soda.

Coconut Catholic School Girl

1 tablespoon honey   3 ounces Coco Lopez
shredded coconut   juice from 1 lime

Dip the rim of a martini glass into the honey and the shredded coconut. Chill the glass in the freezer to add a nice touch. Pour the Coco Lopez and lime juice into a shaker tin of ice. Shake, then strain into the martini glass.

Coffee Almond Float

¼ cup coffee   1 ounce milk
1 teaspoon brown sugar   1 scoop coffee or chocolate ice cream
1 teaspoon almond syrup

Pour all the ingredients except for the scoop of ice cream into a shaker of ice. Shake and strain into a martini glass and top with a scoop of ice cream. Can be served with a spoon.

Cool as a Cucumber

half a peeled cucumber   1 tablespoon sugar or Splenda
juice from half a lime   1 ounce water
2 mint leaves   sprig of mint
half a peeled ripe kiwi

Put all ingredients except mint in a blender. Add ice until you reach a frozen yet pourable consistency. Pour into a martini glass and garnish with mint.

Cranberry and Cream

3 ounces cranberry juice
2 ounces apple juice
1 ounce fresh lime juice

1 ounce cream
dash grenadine

Combine ingredients in a blender with ice. Blend thoroughly. Pour into a tall glass.

Earth Angel Sangria

¾ glass grape juice or nonalcoholic red wine
soda water to fill
orange wheel, lime wheel, pineapple slice, and cherry

Fill a tall glass three-quarters full with grape juice or nonalcoholic red wine. Fill with soda water. Garnish with an orange wheel, lime wheel, pineapple slice, and cherry.

Nonalcoholic Wine

ARIEL is a pioneer in producing award-winning non-alcoholic wines. As a matter of fact, it is the only nonalcoholic wine that won a gold medal against eight alcoholic wines at the Los Angeles County Fair's blind wine tastings.

Creamy Cherry

4 ounces cherry soda
2 scoops vanilla ice cream
1 tablespoon honey
1 ounce cream
dash grenadine

Combine ingredients in a blender without ice. Blend thoroughly. Pour into a tall glass.

Easy Alexander

1 teaspoon instant coffee granules
1 teaspoon brown sugar
1 ounce boiling water
1 ounce cream
sprinkle of nutmeg

Dissolve coffee and sugar in boiling water. Let cool. Combine with cream in a shaker half filled with ice. Shake well and starin into a cocktail glass. Serve with a sprinkle of nutmeg.

Eye of the Hurricane

1 ounce rum extract
2 ounces passion fruit juice

1 ounce fresh lime juice

Combine everything in a shaker tin of ice. Strain over a tall glass of ice.

Faux Kir Royale

1 ounce raspberry syrup
chilled sparkling white grape juice to fill
lemon twist

Pour raspberry syrup into a champagne flute. Fill with sparkling white grape juice. Garnish with a lemon twist.

Frozen Mocha Russian

2 ounces cold black coffee
2 scoops chocolate ice cream

1 ounce cream
sprinkle of chocolate shavings

Combine the first three ingredients in a blender without ice. Blend thoroughly and pour into a tall glass. Top with chocolate shavings.

Good Ship Lollipop

cold Nehi Peach soda to fill
1 large scoop orange sherbet
3 small cantaloupe balls
3 small watermelon balls

Drop a scoop of orange sherbet into the bottom of a tall glass. Fill with cold soda. Drop in the fruit balls. You can replace the orange sherbet with pineapple or lime.

Ancient Sherbet
The Chinese taught Arab traders how to combine syrups and snow to make sherbet. Arab traders showed the Venetians, and the Venetians showed the Romans.

Hairless Reggae

½ banana, sliced
1 ounce fresh orange juice
1 ounce fresh lime juice
½ ounce grenadine
seasonal fruit, chopped

Combine first four ingredients in a blender with a cup of ice. Blend. Pour into a tall glass and garnish with chopped fruit.

Hot Clamato

6 ounces Clamato juice
1 ounce fresh lime juice
¼ teaspoon horseradish

dash Tabasco sauce
dash Worcestershire sauce
lemon wedge

Pour ingredients into a glass over ice; stir. Garnish with lemon.

Tabasco

Tabasco, the popular hot sauce, comes from Avery Island, 140 miles west of New Orleans. It has been produced since 1868. A 2-ounce bottle contains at least 720 drops.

Hot Not Toddy

dash cinnamon
1 tablespoon honey
dash ground cloves

dash nutmeg
6 ounces hot tea
splash lemon juice

In a coffee mug, dissolve the honey and spices in 1 ounce of tea. Stir. Add the lemon juice and the rest of the tea. Stir well.

Italian Cream Soda

1 ounce hazelnut syrup
club soda to fill
whipped cream

Pour hazelnut syrup into a tall glass of ice. Fill with club soda. Top with whipped cream and a straw.

Root Beer Float

It may seem odd to put whipped cream on top of a drink with ice, but it's quite all right. You can use anise extract, cola, and cream over ice, then put whipped cream on top—it will taste like a Root Beer Float.

Juicy Julep

1 ounce fresh lime juice
1 ounce pineapple juice
½ ounce raspberry syrup
2 sprigs of mint (one for garnish)
club soda to fill

Combine the first four ingredients in a shaker half filled with ice. Shake well. Strain into a Collins glass of ice. Add club soda and stir gently. Garnish with a sprig of mint.

Just Say No Cocoa

1 packet cocoa mix
¾ cup hot water

eggnog to fill
whipped cream

Pour a packet of hot cocoa mix in a cup. Fill three-quarters of the way with very hot water and stir well. Fill the rest of the way with eggnog. Top with whipped cream.

Kiss on the Cheek

2 ounces apricot nectar
1 ounce fresh lemon juice

club soda to fill

Pour apricot nectar and lemon juice into a mixing glass nearly filled with ice. Stir well. Strain into a highball glass over ice. Fill with club soda.

Like a Blessed Blackberry Virgin

handful of blackberries
1 teaspoon sugar or Splenda

lemonade to fill
lemon slice and blackberries

Blend the blackberries and sugar or Splenda in a blender until mixed well. Pour into a tall glass. Fill the glass with lemonade and ice. Garnish with a lemon slice and some blackberries.

Lime Cola

1 ounce lime juice or juice of half a lime
cola to fill
lime wedge

Pour lime juice over ice in a highball glass; fill with cola. Garnish with a lime wedge.

Mango Virgo

3 ounces mango nectar
juice from half a lime
2 ounces cream
star fruit

Pour the mango nectar, lime juice, and cream into a shaker tin of ice. Shake and strain into a chilled martini glass and garnish with a star fruit on the rim.

Mimi's Mimosa

2 ounces fresh orange juice
chilled sparkling white grape juice to fill

Pour orange juice into a champagne flute. Fill with sparkling white grape juice.

Morally Pure Mudslide

1 scoop chocolate ice cream
1 scoop vanilla ice cream
1 ounce cold black coffee
2 tablespoons Café Vienna
1 ounce chocolate syrup
milk or cream to blend

Put the chocolate ice cream, vanilla ice cream, coffee, Café Vienna, and chocolate syrup into a blender and blend. Add milk or cream little by little until the mixture reaches a smooth consistency. Pour into a tall glass.

Mulled Cranberry Juice

6 ounces cranberry juice
1 teaspoon honey or
    more to taste
splash of fresh lemon juice
2 whole cloves
dash nutmeg

Combine ingredients in a saucepan and heat to simmer. Do not boil. Stir well. Pour into a coffee mug.

Nada Colada

¼ ounce rum extract
¼ ounce vanilla extract
3 ounces pineapple juice
3 ounces Coco Lopez
milk or cream to blend
pineapple slice and maraschino cherry

Pour the rum extract, vanilla extract, pineapple juice, and Coco Lopez into a blender with a cup of ice. Add milk or cream and blend until the mixture reaches a smooth consistency. Pour into a tall glass and garnish with a pineapple slice and maraschino cherry.

Orange Julius

6 ounces frozen orange juice   1 teaspoon vanilla extract
½ cup of cream

Put everything in a blender with a cup of ice and blend. Pour into a tall glass.

Peaches and Cream

1 peach, chopped   2 ounces light cream
1 teaspoon sugar   peach slice

Combine first three ingredients in a blender with a cup of ice and blend. Pour into a tall glass and garnish with a slice of peach.

Georgia Peach

Georgia is known for many things, but the most beloved is the Georgia peach. Peaches originated in Asia. Persians brought the peach to Persia and then introduced to them to Italy. The Italians introduced them to Spain, and then Spanish explorers brought them to Georgia. The Georgia peach industry began during Reconstruction after the American Civil War. Today, more than 40 varieties of peaches are grown in Georgia.

Pineapple Twist

4 ounces pineapple juice
1 ounce lemon juice or juice of half a lemon
2 ounces orange juice or juice of half an orange
maraschino cherry

Combine juices in a blender with ice. Blend thoroughly. Pour into a cocktail glass and serve with a cherry.

Pink Pineapple

4 ounces pineapple juice
3 ounces cherry soda
1 tablespoon honey

1 ounce cream
dash grenadine

Pour into a tall glass of ice. Stir.

Nonalcoholic Planter's Punch

2 ounces pineapple juice
3 ounces fresh orange juice
1 ounce fresh lemon juice
½ ounce grenadine
fruit

Combine all liquid ingredients in a shaker half filled with ice. Shake well. Strain into a tall glass of ice. Garnish with fruit. This is the nonalcoholic version of the rum-flavored punch of the same name.

Pomegranate Lemonade

1 ounce pomegranate syrup
lemonade to fill

Pour the pomegranate syrup in a tall glass of ice and fill with lemonade.

Pure Polynesian Pepper Pot

4 ounces pineapple juice
½ ounce almond syrup
1 ounce fresh lemon juice
4 dashes Tabasco
dash curry powder

Combine the first four ingredients in a shaker half filled with ice. Shake well. Strain into a tall glass of ice. Sprinkle curry on top.

Quiet Passion

3 ounces white grape juice
3 ounces grapefruit juice
1 ounce passion fruit juice

Combine ingredients in a shaker half filled with ice. Shake well. Strain into a tall glass of ice.

Raspberry Cloud

¼ cup raspberries, fresh or frozen
1 ounce milk
1 tablespoon honey

Put berries in a blender and blend well. Add milk, honey, and two ice cubes. Pour into a tall glass.

Reno Cocktail

2 ounces grapefruit juice
1 ounce lime juice or juice of half a lime
½ ounce grenadine
1 teaspoon fine sugar

Combine ingredients in a shaker nearly filled with ice. Strain into a cocktail glass.

Safe Sex on the Beach

1 ounce Torani or Monin peach syrup
equal parts orange juice and cranberry juice to fill
orange slice and cherry

Pour the peach syrup into a tall glass of ice. Fill with equal parts orange juice and cranberry juice. Garnish with orange slice and cherry.

Salty Puppy

lime wedge
coarse salt
4 to 5 ounces grapefruit juice

Rub the rim of a tall glass with the lime wedge. Pour the salt into a dish and dip the rim of the glass into the mixture. Add ice and pour in grapefruit juice.

Slumbering Bull

5 ounces V8 juice
2 ounces beef bouillon
dash Tabasco
dash Worcestershire sauce
dash celery salt
lime wedge

Pour all liquid ingredients and celery salt into a highball glass over ice and stir well. Garnish with a lime wedge.

Sunshine State

4 ounces cherry soda
½ cup orange sherbet
1 ounce fresh lemon juice

Combine ingredients in a blender with ice. Blend well. Pour into a tall glass.

Sweet Sunrise

orange juice to fill
½ ounce grenadine
orange slice

Fill a tall glass with ice; then fill with orange juice. Slowly pour the grenadine into the drink. It will sink to the bottom of the glass, making it look like a sunrise. Garnish with an orange slice.

Touched by a Fuzzy Angel

1 ounce peach syrup
orange juice to fill
orange or peach slice

Pour the peach syrup into a tall glass of ice. Fill with orange juice, and garnish with fruit. Basically, it's a Virgin Fuzzy Navel.

Vice Presidente

2 ounces pineapple juice
1 ounce lime juice or juice of half a lime
½ ounce grenadine
1 teaspoon fine sugar

Combine ingredients in a shaker nearly filled with ice. Strain into a cocktail glass. This is a virgin version of the rum-flavored El Presidente.

Virgin Island Seabreeze

1 part pink grapefruit juice
1 part cranberry juice

lime slice

Fill a tall glass with ice. Pour in equal amounts of the pink grapefruit juice and cranberry juice. Garnish with a slice of lime.

Wild Blueberry Beginner

5 mint leaves
handful of blueberries
1 tablespoon sugar or Splenda

1 ounce water
7-Up to fill
sprig of mint and blueberries

Put the first four ingredients into a tall glass. Mash all the ingredients together with a muddler or wooden spoon to release the oils in the mint. Fill the glass with ice and 7-Up and garnish with mint and blueberries.

Appendix A

The Wrath of Grapes— All about Hangovers

The buzz from drinking alcohol can be compared to the high an addictive shopper feels from a day of credit-card shopping. The hangover happens the next day when you realize you have to pay.

The Top Five Hangover Preventions

After drinking, the most common prevention is to take aspirin and drink a big glass of water before going to sleep. What you want to take is ibuprofen and water. Tylenol (acetaminophen) causes extreme liver damage when combined with alcohol.

1. Drink water while drinking alcohol
2. Snack while drinking
3. Drink high-quality alcohol
4. Take vitamin B-complex and vitamin C
5. Take ibuprofen.

The Top Five Hangover Cures

There has never been one cure-all for a hangover the day after. As you can imagine, there are thousands upon thousands of common folk hangover cures that have been passed down from generation to generation. There are also modern-day powders and potions that claim to be the cure-all. You'll just have to determine what is best for you.

1. The Hair of the Dog. This refers to drinking a bit more alcohol to cure you. Supposedly the term has been around since the 1500s and refers to placing a few dog hairs over a dog's bite wound to cure the wound. Somehow it evolved into a drinking metaphor.

2. Drinking a Bloody Mary is considered a classic hangover cure, especially when you add hot sauce, an egg, lemon juice, and other ingredients to the mix.

3. Drinking PowerAde or Gatorade will supposedly rehydrate the body with essential nutrients.

4. Eat raw egg yolks because they are high in cysteine (SIS-tuh-een). There is also an over-the-counter supplement called N-aceltycysteine (NAC).

5. A hot bath or shower is supposed to help you sweat out the toxins from the alcohol. If you are feeling very uneasy, have someone nearby to help you back in bed.

Global Hangover Cures

As you can imagine, there are as many hangover cures around the world as there are ways to get rid of the hiccups.

- **America circa 1800:** Soak feet in mustard and eat eggs Benedict.
- **Ancient Egypt:** Eat boiled cabbage.
- **Ancient Romans:** Eat fried canary.
- **England:** Have clam chowder.
- **France:** Eat or drink hot onion soup.
- **Germany:** Have pickled herring with a beer.
- **Haiti:** Stick thirteen black-headed pins in the cork of the bottle you drank from.
- **Ireland:** Have an Ulster Fry (potato bread, fried egg, bacon, sausage, tomato, mushrooms, and soda bread).
- **Japan:** Wear a sake-soaked surgical mask.
- **Puerto Rico:** Rub a lemon under your drinking arm.
- **Russia:** Have salted cucumber juice or black bread soaked in water.

Appendix B

Drinking Words Through Time

These won't help you win a trivia contest, but they will make you chuckle.

1300s: Drunk as a whistle, drunk as all get-out, taverned, cupshotten, down among the dead men, drunk as an ape, dizzy, feebleminded, mad, double-tongued, drunk as a mouse, drunk as a Pope.

1400s: Drowned the shamrock, dronke, drunk as a swine, overseen, pissed as a skunk, served up, off me pickle, aroused.

1500s: Aled up, befuddled, drinking deep, malt above the meal, swallowed a tavern token, shattered, shaved, swilled up, whittled, rowdy, has more than one can hold, has on a barley cap.

1600s: Admiral of the narrow seas, beastly drunk, cap-sick, bubbled, caught a fox, D and D (drunk and disorderly), boozed, dull in the eye, elevated, giggled up, got bread and cheese in one's head, muddled up, drinking merry-go-round, on the rampage, seeing double.

1700s: Addled, rotten drunk, cherry-merry, clips the King's English, cracked, cranked, dizzy as a coot, fuddled up, full as a goat, got a snootful, groggy, happy-juiced, in the altitudes, jacked up, juiced to the gills, lapping it up, cockadoodled, drinking like a fish, and stewed, screwed, and tattooed.

1800s: A bit on, a couple of chapters into the novel, a cup too much, a date with John Barleycorn, a drop too much, a little in the suds, peg too low, piece of bread and cheese in the attic, a public mess, on a bender, above par, altogether drunk, apple palsy, at peace with the floor, lifting the little finger, been looking through a glass, banged up on sauce, bemused, blue around the gills, breath strong enough to carry coal with, can't see a hole in a ladder, caught the flavor, corked, dead to the world, doped up, woozy, drunk as Bacchus, drunk as forty billygoats, electrified, feeling glorious, fired up, fogged in, full to the brim, ginned, groggified, half gone, haywire, inked, lushed, moonshined, off the deep end, on the rocks, pie-eye, polished, sloppy drunk, sloshed, stinking, soaked, swazzled, tanked, whacked out of one's skull.

1900s: Lit, high, party animal, three sheets to the wind, tipsy, slave to drink, aboard, blown away, done, gone, liquored up, bashed, buzzed, acting like a fool, baked, blasted, bombed, blitzed, bonkers, canned, creamed, crocked, fried, hammered, stoned, toasted, double vision, wasted.

2000s: Boneless, get the fade on, tight, torqued, bulletproof, shined, Picassoed, locked out of your mind, jagged up, in the paint, pixilated, punch drunk, drunk as hell.

Index

57 Chevy, 216
57 Chevy with Hawaiian License
  Plates, 217

A

Acapulco Clam Digger, 154
Acapulco Zombie, 217
Ace of Spades, 182
Ace of Spades (Casino Party
  Martini), 238
Ace Ventura, 217
Adam and Eve, 217
Adirondack Mint, 69
Admiral Nelson's Brew, 132
Affair, 69
Affinity, 173
After Five, 70
Afternoon Delight, 70
Agent Orange, 181
Aggravation, 173
AK-47, 218
Alabama Slammer, 218
Alabama Slammer Shot, 193
Alamo, 155
Alamo PowWow, 155
Alaska, 112
Ale Punch, 35
Alexander, 113
Algonquin, 181

All American, 181
Almond Joy, 70
Almond Joytini, 133
Aloha, 218
Alpine Lemonade, 219
Alternatini, 219
Amaretto, 257
Ambrosia, 58–59
Americana, 182
American Cobbler, 182
Americano, 71
Angel's Fall, 219
Angel's Share, 60
Anita Rita Now, 155
Anna Banana, 273
Apple Ginger Gin, 113
Apple Pie, 219
Apricot Sour, 59
Armagnac Lillet, 71
Around the World, 220
Astro Pop, 203
Autumn in New York, 251
Aviation, 113
Aztec Gold, 155

B

B&B, 59
B-52, 203
Baby Bellini, 273

Baby Doll, 59
Baby Shower Champagne, 238
Bacardi Cocktail, 133
Bachelorette Strip and Go Naked
  Punch, 239
Bahama Mama, 133
Bailey's Comet, 209
Balloon Wine, 257
Balmoral, 173
Banana Boat, 133
Banana Daiquiri, 134
Banana Jack, 193
Banana Popsicle, 134
Banshee, 71
Barbary Coast, 220
Barmarche Honey Sour, 89
Baronial, 72
Bar Punch, 258
Basic Bitters, 258
Baybreeze, 89
Bazooka Joe, 193
Beam Me Up, Scotty, 193
Beautiful, 59
Beer Belly Margarita, 156
Beer Buster, 36
Bee's Knees, 113
Bee Sting, 36
Belgian Brownie, 114
Bellini, 53
Bermuda Rose, 114
Bermuda Triangle Tea, 134
Berry Bordello, 89
Between the Hotel Sheets
  Margarita, 156
Between the Sheets, 60, 135

Big as the MoonPie, 273
Big Banana!, 220
Bijou, 114
Bionic Tonic, 220–21
Bird of Paradise, 156
Bishop, 49
Bittersweet Cocktail, 73
Black and Tan, 36
Blackberry Mojito, 135
Blackberry Zima, 36
Black Death, 193
Black Goose, 89
Black Honey, 72
Black Magic, 90
Black Maria, 221
Black Martini, 90
Black Rose, 204
Black Russian, 72
Black Slippery Nipple, 204
Black Thorn, 178
Black Velvet, 36, 54
Blarney Stone, 178
Blinded by the Light Girly
  Birthday Drink, 240
Blinder, 174
Bloody Beer, 37
Bloody Caesar, 90
Bloody Maria, 156
Bloody Mary, 90–91
Bloody Mary Mix, 259
Blow Job, 204
Blow My Skull Off, 37
Blue Balls, 194
Blue Blazer, 174
Blue Hawaiian, 135

Blue Hawaiian Shake, 274
Blue Knickers, 221
Blue Lagoon, 91
Blue Marlin Shooter, 198
Blue Skyy Summer, 248
Blue Velvetini, 221
Blue Voodoo Doll, 157
Blushin' Berry Mary, 274
Bobby Burns, 175
Boilermaker, 37, 212
Bolero, 222
Bolo, 136
Bombay Cocktail, 61
Bon Bon, 136
Booming Gin, 115
Born on the 4th of July Martini, 248
Boston Sidecar, 222
Bourbon and Branch, 182
Bourbon Daisy, 183
Bourbon on the Rocks, 183
Bourbon Satin, 183
Brain Hemorrhage, 194
Bramble, 115
Brandy Alexander, 60
Brandy Cassis, 61
Brandy Manhattan, 61
Brandy Milk Punch, 61
Brandy Vermouth Classic, 61
Brass Monkey, 222
Brave Bull, 157
Brazilian Breakfast, 136
Broadway, 38
Broken Down Golf Cart, 198
Bronx, 115

Bull and Bear, 183
Bull Dog, 115
Bull Shot, 91
Burning Bush, 212
Bushwacker, 137
Butterscotch Coffee, 73
Buttery Nipple, 204

C

Cabaret Cocktail, 116
Cactus Bite, 157
Caipirinha, 137
Caipiroska, 92
California Lemonade, 184
Calvados Cocktail, 62
Canadian Cherry, 184
Canadian Cocktail, 184
Canadian Crown, 249
Candy Corn, 204
Cape Codder/Cape Cod, 92
Captain's Blood, 137
Captain's Stripes, 205
Caramel Appletini, 73
Cardinal, 49
Caribbean Eclipse, 137
Caribbean Night, 38
Cement Mixer, 198
Champagne and Chambord, 54
Champagne Antoine, 54
Champagne Cocktail, 55
Champagne Fizz or Diamond Fizz, 55
Champagne Flamingo, 55
Champagne Mint, 55

Charming Proposal, 74
Charro Negro, 157
Chatham Artillery Punch, 249
Cheeky Tractor, 38
Cherry Blossom, 222
Cherry Coke, 274
Chi-Chi, 92
Chinese New Year Champagne, 244
Chiquita, 93
Chocolate Cake, 194
Chocolate Coco, 137
Chocolate Dipped Strawberry, 274
Chocolate Monkey, 74
Chocolate Pudding Pop, 93
Cigar Band, 205
Cinco De Mayo Martini, 250
Clover Club, 116
Coconut Brownie with Nuts, 93
Coconut Catholic School Girl, 275
Coconut Concubine, 94
Coffee Almond Float, 275
Coffee Liqueur, 259–60
Coffee Nudge, 65
Colonial Cocktail, 116
Colorado Bulldog, 74
Combustible Edison, 62
Come Hither, 74
Compadre, 158
Continental, 223
Cool as a Cucumber, 275
Copabanana Split, 94
Coral Snake Bite, 205

Corkscrew, 223
Corona Limon, 38
Coronation, 74
Corona with Training Wheels, 38
Corpse Reviver, 223
Cortés, 75
Cosmopolitan, 95
Cotton Gin, 116
Cowboy Martini, 116–17
Cranberry and Cream, 276
Cranberry Cosmorita, 158
Cranberry Juice, 259
Creamsicle, 95
Creamy Cherry, 276
Creamy Mocha Alexander, 62
Cuba Libre (Rum and Cake), 138

D

Daiquiri, 138
Dark 'n Stormy, 138
Death by Chocolatini, 95
Death in the Afternoon, 55
Delovely, 63
Depth Charge, 39
Derby Cocktail, 117
Devil's Blood, 252
Diablo Cocktail, 75
Diamond Fizz, 55
Dirty Girl Scout Cookie, 96
Dirty Martini, 117
Dirty Mother, 63
Dirty White Mother, 63
Distressed Damson, 117
Divorce Party Blues, 240

Dixie Whiskey, 224
Dog's Bollocks, 39
Downsider, 158
Dragon's Breath, 209
Dream Cocktail, 63
Dr. Pepper, 39
Drunken Olives, 260
Dry Negroni, 75
Dry Tea, 118
Dubonnet Cocktail, 76
Dubonnet Rouge, 76
Dutch Breakfast, 118
Dutchie, 224
Dutch Trade Winds, 118
Dynamite, 158

E

Earth Angel Sangria, 276
Easter Egg, 206
Easy Alexander, 277
Eggnog, 260–61
Eggnog Grog, 138
El Chico, 224
El Diablo, 159
Electric Iced Tea, 225
El Niño, 159
El Presidente, 225
Embassy Cocktail, 225
Eternal Flame, 209
Eye of the Hurricane, 277

F

Fancy Brandy, 64
Faux Absinthe, 261

Faux Aquavit, 261–62
Faux Drambuie, 262
Faux Galliano, 262
Faux Kir Royale, 277
Faux Pimm's No. 1, 263
Feliz Natal, 225
First Kiss, 139
Flaming Dr. Pepper, 212
Flamingo, 139
Flat Tire at the Border, 159
Flavored/Infused Spirits, 263
Flexible Ice Pack, 263–64
Flirtini, 56
Floradora, 119
Florida Sunset, 96
Florida Sunshine Beer, 40
Floridita, 225
Fog Cutter, 226
Foggy Afternoon, 226
Forbidden Fruit, 139
Foreign Affair, 76
Freddy Fudpucker, 159
French 75, 56, 119
French Martini, 119
French Passion, 64
Frog in a Blender, 76
Frozen Girl Scout Cookie, 77
Frozen Mocha Russian, 277
Fuzzy Navel, 77

G

Garden Party Sangria (white
    sangria with rose petals), 240
Gentlemen's Cocktail, 185

Georgia Peach, 96
Georgia Rose, 97
Gibson, 119
Gimlet, 120
Gin and It, 120
Gin and Juice, 120
Gin and Sin, 120
Gin and Tonic, 120
Gin Daisy, 121
Gin Fizz, 121
Ginger Beer, 264
Gingered Apple, 139
Gin Rickey, 121
Gin Sour, 121
Glogg, 49
God Bless Texastini, 160
Godfather, 78, 175
Godmother, 78
Goin' Coconutini, 140
Golden Cadillac, 78
Golden Friendship, 226
Good Karma, 78
Good Ship Lollipop, 278
Grasshopper, 78
Green, Gold, and Purple, 247
Green Beer, 245
Green-Eyed Blonde, 79
Green-Eyed Irish Blonde, 206
Green Iguana, 160
Greyhound, 97
The Grinch's Sour Caramel Apple
    Pie, 252

H

Habla Español Fly, 160
Hairless Reggae, 278
Hairy Navel, 97
Hand Grenade, 226
Harvey Wallbanger, 98
Hawaiian Iced Tea, 227
Hawaiian Luau Jungle Juice, 241
Hawaiian Volcano, 140
Hemingway Daiquiri, 140
Holly Berry, 252
Hollywood, 98
Honeymoon Cocktail, 227
Honeymoon Suite, 79
Horny Margarita, 160
Horse's Neck, 250
Hot Apple Pie, 210
Hot Beer, 40
Hot Blooded, 210
Hot Buttered Rum, 140
Hot Buttered Rum Mix, 265
Hot Buttered Sugarplum Rum,
    141
Hot Clamato, 278
Hot Gingerbread Toddy, 141
Hot Not Toddy, 279
Housewarming Sangria, 241–42
Huckleberry Finn Gin, 122
Hunka Hunka Burning Love, 98
Hurricane, 141
Hypnotizing Margarita, 161

I

Ice Palace, 227
I Dream of Genie Martini, 98–99
Instant Cappuccino Mocha Mix, 265
In the Mood, 142
Irish Car Bomb, 178, 213
Irish Coffee, 178
Irish Cream, 266
Irish Magic, 179
Irish Rickey, 179
Irish Shannigan, 228
Irish Shillelagh, 179
Isar Water, 40
Italian Breeze, 142
Italian Cream Soda, 279
Itsy Bitsy Teenie Weenie Yellow Polka Dot Martini, 99

J

Jack Be Nimble Java, 185
Jack Black, 206
Jack Rose, 64
Jäger Bomb, 213
Jalisco Smash, 161
Jamaican Me Crazy, 142
Jasmine, 122
Jelly Bean, 195
John Collins, 185
Jolly Roger, 142
J. R.'s Godfather, 185
Juicy Julep, 280
Jumping Beans, 162

Jupiter Cocktail, 122
Just Say No Cocoa, 280

K

Kama Sutra, 245
Kama Sutra Martini, 64
Kamikaze, 198
Kentucky Colonel, 186
Keoke Coffee, 65
Key Lime Pie Margarita, 162
K.G.B., 228
Kir, 49
Kir Royale, 56
Kiss from a Rosarita, 162
Kiss from a Rose, 246
Kiss on the Cheek, 280
Knickerbocker, 142–43

L

La Bomba, 163
Lady's Cocktail, 186
Lager and Lime, 41
Las Vegas, Baby!, 228
Latitude Attitude Adjuster, 143
Lava Colada, 143
Lemon Chiffon Pie, 143
Lemondrop Martini, 100
Lemon Drop Shooter, 199
Lemon Drop Shot, 195
Lemon Love Shack Shake, 100
Lemon Raspberry Rita, 163
Like a Blessed Blackberry Virgin, 280

Lime Cola, 281
Limoncello, 264
Liquid Cocaine, 195
Liquid Viagra, 100
Liverpool Kiss, 41
Lolita, 163
Long Beach Tea, 228
Long Island Iced Tea, 229
Looney Bin Gin, 123
Lounge Lizard, 144
Love Potion, 80
Love Potion #9, 100
Lucky Charm, 80
Lunch Box, 213
Lynchburg Lemonade, 186

M

Madras, 101
Magnum, 229
Mai Tai Me Up, 144
Mango Heat Wave, 101
Mango Virgo, 281
Manhattan, 186
Man Hunting, 229
Man O' War, 187
Margarita, 164
Martinez, 123
Martini, 123
Mary Pickford, 144
Mead, 266
Melon Ball, 101
Melonliscious Mistress, 102
Melon Mimosa, 56
Metropolitan, 102

Mexican Cherry, 41
Mexican Flag, 206
Mexican Madras, 164
Mexican Moonlight, 164
Miami Iced Tea, 230
Michelada, 41
Millionaire, 187
Million-Dollar Cocktail, 124
Mimi's Mimosa, 281
Mimosa, 57
Mind Eraser, 199
Mint Bourbon, 266
Mint Julep, 187
Mint Julep Punch, 250
Modern Cocktail, 175
Mojito, 145
Mojo, 230
Monkey Gland, 124
Monkey's Lunch, 199
Montezuma, 165
Moonlight Drive, 230
Morally Pure Mudslide, 282
Moscow Mule, 102
Mudslide, 102
Mudslide Martini, 231
Mulled Cranberry Juice, 282
Mulled Wine, 50
Muy Bonita Rita, 165

N

Nada Colada, 282
Naked Twister, 231
Napoleon, 62
Navy Grogg, 145

Neapolitan Martini, 231
Negroni, 80, 124
Ninja Turtle, 124
Nonalcoholic Planter's Punch, 284
Nuts and Berries, 80
Nutty Irishman, 81
Nutty Irishman-tini, 246

O

Oatmeal Cookie, 195
Old-Fashioned, 188
Old Pal, 188
Olympia, 145
Orange Julius, 283
Orange Spiked Lager, 42
Orgasm, 81
Orgasm Shooter, 199
Original Red Snapper, 127

P

Paddy Cocktail, 179
Painkiller, 146
Paradise Under a Coconut Tree, 146
Passion Beer, 42
Passion Cup, 103
PB&J, 232
PB&J with Bananas, 232
Peaches and Cream, 283
Peaches and Creamtini, 103
Peaches at the Beaches, 146
Peach Purée, 267

Peach Spiked Brew, 42
Peanut Butter and Jelly, 195
Pearl Harbor, 103
Pegu Club, 125
Peppermint Pattie, 81
Perfect Rob Roy, 175
Petroleo, 165
Picon Fizz, 82
Pimm's Cup, 82
Pimm's Royale, 57
Piña Colada, 146
Piñata, 166
Pineapple Mist, 147
Pineapple Mojito, 147
Pineapple Twist, 283
Pineapple Upside-Down Birthday Cake, 241
Pink Cadillactini, 104
Pink Gin, 125
Pink Lady, 125
Pink Pajama Party Shots, 242
Pink Pineapple, 284
Pink Squirrel, 82
Pirates Sour, 126
Pirate's Treasure, 207
Planter's Punch, 147
Platinum Blonde Coffee, 82
Poinsettia, 57
Polar Bear, 196
Pomegranate Lemonade, 284
Pomegranate Martini, 104
Prairie Fire Shooter, 196
Pumpkin Pie, 253
Pure Polynesian Pepper Pot, 284

Purple Hooter, 200

Q

Queen Elizabeth, 82
Queen Stinger, 188
Quiet Passion, 285

R

Ragin' Cajun Mardi Gras Punch,
   246
Ramos Gin Fizz, 126
Raspberry Cloud, 285
Raspberry Collins, 126
Raspberry Lemon Drop, 200
Raspberry Liqueur, 267
Raspberry Long Island Ice Tea,
   232
Red Death, 232
Red Eye, 43
Redheaded Slut, 200
Red-Headed Stepchild, 42
Red Snapper, 200
Reno Cocktail, 285
Rhinestone Dallas Cowboy, 207
Rimmed Brothers Grimm Cocoa,
   65
Rob Roy, 176
Rockapolitan, 148
Root Beer Float, 83
Ruby, 43
Ruby Slipper, 83
Rum Runner, 148
Russian Quaalude, 196
Russian Spring Punch, 104

Rusty Nail, 176
Rusty Windmill, 127
Rye and Ginger, 189

S

Safe Sex on the Beach, 285
Sake Bomb, 43
Sake to Me, 214
Salma Hayek, 166
Salty Dog, 104
Salty Puppy, 286
Sambuca, 83
Sammy Jäger, 197
Sangria #1, 50
Sangria #2, 267–68
Satan's Whiskers, 233
Sazerac, 189
Scarlett O'Hara, 84
Schnapps, 268
Scorpion, 148
Scotch and Milk, 176
Scotch and Soda, 176
Scotch Holiday Sour, 176
Scotch Mist, 176
Scotch on the Rocks, 177
Scotch Sour, 177
Screaming Orgasm, 201
Screwdriver, 105
Seabreeze, 105
Selena, 166
Separator, 65
Seven and Seven, 188
Sex in Front of the Fireplace, 105
Sex on the Beach, 106

Sex on the Farm, 233
Sex with the Captain, 148
Sexy Alligator, 201
Shady Lady, 166
Shalom, 233
Shamrock, 179
Shandy, 43
Shore Breeze, 127
Showshoe, 201
Sidecar, 66
Silk Panty, 207
Silk Stocking, 166
Simple Syrup, 268
Singapore Sling, 127
Singapore Sling #2, 128
Skip and Go Naked, 43, 128
Skippy, 44
Slippery Dick, 208
Slippery Nipple, 208
Sloe Comfortable Fuzzy Screw
   Against the Wall, 233
Sloe Comfortable Screw, 233
Sloe Comfortable Screw Against
   the Wall, 234
Sloe Comfortable Screw Against
   the Wall in Mexico, 234
Sloe Comfortable Screw Between
   the Sheets, 234
Sloe Screw, 106
Slumbering Bull, 286
Smiling Tiger, 106
Smith & Kearns, 84
Smith & Wesson, 84
S'Mores, 211
Snake Bite, 201

Snake in the Apple Tree, 44
Sneaky Pete, 44
SoCo, 190
SoCo and Lime, 201
Sombrero, 84
Sonata, 66
Sonora, 149
Sour Apple-tini, 107
Southern Hospitality, 84
Southern Lady, 189
South of the Peachy Border Rita, 167
South Wind, 44
Spanish Moss, 167
Spa Party Martini, 244
Sparkling New Year Cheer, 247
Spiced Beer, 44
Spiced Cider, 269
Spicy Pear, 149
Statue of Liberty, 211
Stinger, 66
Stop Light, 202
Stork Club Cocktail, 128
Straits Sling, 128
Strawberry Daiquiri, 149
Strawberry Mojitorita, 167
Strike's On, 129
Stupid Cupid, 107
Sugar and Spice and Everything
   Nice, 45
Summertime Slushy, 251
Sunbathing on a Mexican Beach,
   167
Sunshine State, 286
Super Bowl Drop Kick, 247
Surfer on Acid, 202

Sweet-and-Sour/Margarita Mix, 269

Sweet Sunrise, 286

Sweet Vermouth on the Rocks, 85

Swim-Up Bar Margarita, 168

T

Tango, 235

Tasting Away in Margaritaville, 168

T-Bird, 190

Tequila Mockingbird Margarita, 169

Tequila Slammer, 202

Tequila Sunrise, 168

Tequila Sunrise Margarita, 169

Texas Ex's, 235

Texas Tea, 235

Tezón Caramel Apple Pie, 169

Thanksgiving Turkey Cosmo, 253

Thin Gin, 129

Think Pink, 150

Thorny Mexican, 169

Three Señoritas Margarita, 235

Three Wise Men, 197

Three Wise Men Go Hunting, 197

Three Wise Men Visit Mexico, 197

Toasted Almond, 85

Tomahawk, 45

Tom Collins, 129

Tootsie Roll, 85

Tootsie Roll Shooter, 202

Toreador, 170

Touched by a Fuzzy Angel, 287

Tropical Beer, 46

Tropical Rain Forest, 236

Truffle, 150

Twentieth Century, 236

U

Upside-Down Pineapple Martini, 107

V

Valentine, 50

Vermouth Cassis, 86

Vesper, 236

Vice Presidente, 287

Vino Crush, 51

Virgin Island Seabreeze, 287

Vodka and Tonic, 108

Vodka Collins, 108

Vodka Gimlet, 108

Vodka Martini, 109

Vodka on the Rocks, 109

Vodka Red Bull, 109

Vodka Sour, 109

W

Waldorf, 236

Ward 8, 190

Washington Apple, 202

Wassail, 253

Wedding Cake Martini, 243